Redeeming
Power

Understanding Authority and Abuse in the Church

Diane Langberg

Brazos Press

a division of Baker Publishing Group
Grand Rapids, Michigan

© 2020 by Diane Langberg

Published by Brazos Press
a division of Baker Publishing Group
PO Box 6287, Grand Rapids, MI 49516-6287
www.brazospress.com

Printed in the United States of America

Library of Congress Cataloging-in-Publication Data
Names: Langberg, Diane, author.
Title: Redeeming power : understanding authority and abuse in the church / Diane Langberg.
Description: Grand Rapids, Michigan : Brazos Press, a division of Baker Publishing Group, 2020.
Identifiers: LCCN 2020018324 | ISBN 9781587434389 (paperback) | ISBN 9781587435133 (casebound)
Subjects: LCSH: Power (Christian theology) | Authority—Religious aspects—Christianity. | Offenses against the person.
Classification: LCC BT738.25 .L36 2020 | DDC 261—dc23
LC record available at https://lccn.loc.gov/2020018324

Unless otherwise indicated, Scripture quotations are the author's paraphrase.

Scripture quotations labeled ESV are from The Holy Bible, English Standard Version.® (ESV®) Copyright © 2001 by Crossway, a publishing ministry of Good News Publishers. All rights reserved. Text Edition: 2016.

Scripture quotations labeled KJV are from the King James Version of the Bible.

Scripture quotations labeled NASB are from the New American Standard Bible. Copyright © 1960, 1962, 1963, 1968, 1971, 1972, 1973, 1975, 1977, 1995 by The Lockman Foundation.

Scripture quotations labeled NIV are from the Holy Bible, New International Version®, NIV® Copyright ©1973, 1978, 1984, 2011 by Biblica, Inc.™ Used by permission of Zondervan. All rights reserved worldwide. www.zondervan.com. The "NIV" and "New International Version" are trademarks registered in the United States Patent and Trademark Office by Biblica, Inc.™

Scripture quotations labeled NKJV are from the New King James Version®. Copyright © 1982 by Thomas Nelson. Used by permission. All rights reserved.

Scripture quotations labeled NLT are from the Holy Bible, New Living Translation, copyright © 1996, 2004, 2015 by Tyndale House Foundation. Used by permission of Tyndale House Publishers, Inc., Carol Stream, Illinois 60188. All rights reserved.

Scripture quotations labeled NRSV are from the New Revised Standard Version of the Bible, copyright © 1989 National Council of the Churches of Christ in the United States of America. Used by permission. All rights reserved worldwide.

Composite Disclaimer: The names and details of the people and situations described in this book have been changed or presented in composite form in order to ensure the privacy of those with whom the author has worked.

In keeping with biblical principles of creation stewardship, Baker Publishing Group advocates the responsible use of our natural resources. As a member of the Green Press Initiative, our company uses recycled paper when possible. The text paper of this book is composed in part of post-consumer waste.

21   22   23   24   25   26   7   6   5   4

"With the clear-eyed assessment of Jeremiah and the courage of Esther, Langberg looks leaders square in the eye and tells the unflinching truth about power. This is difficult truth that every leader needs to know but most work hard to avoid. Her relentless pursuit of protecting the powerless is supported by her decades of listening for God's voice amid victims' pain, as well as that of the perpetrators, some of whom don't realize the damage their words and actions produce. For all who hunger for healing and yearn to know how power can be both abused and properly used, this book is for you."

—**Robert L. Briggs**, president and CEO,
American Bible Society

"With immeasurable insight and grace, *Redeeming Power* exhorts people, institutions, and nations to wake up, repent, and seek the kingdom of God by looking critically at the imbalances and injustices we have allowed to flourish. If there was ever a time we needed to receive this challenging, life-saving word, it's now. Thank God for choosing Diane to profess it!"

—**Jeanne L. Allert**, founder and executive director,
The Samaritan Women

"This book broke my heart, instructed my soul, and pointed me to the most powerful King-Servant-Healer, who lovingly humbled himself to overcome evil with good. This is an anointed book, reflecting theological sensitivity and egregious life experiences, calling us to steward and reclaim power for its original purpose: human flourishing."

—**Ronald A. Matthews**, president, Eastern University

"Every now and then you come across a resource that you passionately want to recommend to others because you know its contents are that essential and valuable. *Redeeming Power* is one of those resources. Langberg helps us see and understand the truths we so often miss, ignore, or explain away because they are shrouded in much deception of self and others. *Redeeming Power* is a ray of light streaming through systems and hearts darkened by the abuse of authority. Those who read will discover truths that can reveal, free, and heal."

—**Wade Mullen**, Capital Seminary & Graduate School; author
of *Something's Not Right: Decoding the Hidden Tactics of
Abuse—and Freeing Yourself from Its Power*

"Langberg has done us all an excellent service with this book. There is currently a desperate need within the church to better understand power dynamics. The cost of the church not fully grasping what power is and how it is appropriately stewarded is too high. I see this regularly as I care for those who have endured both spiritual abuse and racial trauma within the church. This book is profound yet accessible and carries with it the potential to inform and heal. I commend it wholeheartedly to all."

—**Kyle J. Howard**, Soul Care Provider, Lighting a Path, Inc.

"The most difficult aspect of my profession is seeing the pain and suffering that people can inflict on each other, especially in church and family environments that should be safe and protective. Dr. Langberg has spent decades understanding what the process of healing from personal and systemic trauma looks like. Her book is required reading for anyone who seeks substantial training in helping victims of emotional, sexual, physical, and racial trauma."

—**Michael R. Lyles, MD**, psychiatrist, speaker, and visiting lecturer

"In this weighty and timely book, Dr. Langberg addresses a topic that too often goes ignored or even dismissed: power. As human beings, we have been given power and that power can be used to serve or to oppress. You will need to read this book with a highlighter and a box of tissues nearby. As a tender and experienced therapist, Langberg writes a book that painfully reveals even as it lovingly heals."

—**Jemar Tisby**, *New York Times* bestselling author of *The Color of Compromise*

"No stodgy academic language here—Langberg is a *woman on fire*, and in a manner worthy of the prophets before her, she delivers a call for justice on behalf of those deeply wounded by power wielded in ungodly ways. This book is packed with biblical truths, insight, wisdom, conviction, and instruction for those who have eyes to see and ears to hear."

—**Kay Warren**, co-founder, Saddleback Church

With love and gratitude to
my father, William F. Mandt,
my father-in-law, Simon Langberg,
my husband, Ronald Langberg,
and our sons, Joshua and Daniel Langberg,
extraordinary men, each distinguished for using their power
with endless kindness and impeccable integrity

Contents

Contents

Part 3   Power Redeemed

Prelude

Decades ago, when I first encountered victims of sexual abuse, I found myself in a foreign land. I did not know such things happened. It was not part of my experience, nor was it mentioned once in the psychological literature I read or while I earned two graduate degrees. The church dismissed me when I brought it up. I decided, by God's grace, to listen to the unbelieved and disenfranchised. Doing so has changed me and shaped my life.

My learning curve over the past forty-seven years as a Christian psychologist has been steep and long. I first learned about families in which sexual and domestic abuse were rampant and had been for generations. I have since sat with victims of trauma, violence, rape, and war. I have learned about people groups who have been crushed, oppressed, and enslaved. I have borne witness to this devastation in my Pennsylvania office and across six continents. I have listened to voices from Auschwitz, Rwanda, South Africa, Congo, and Cambodia while visiting death camps, churches full of bones, places of unspeakable poverty, victims of violent rape, and the Killing Fields, where *human beings were destroyed just because they were who God created them to be.*

I have also seen beauty, redemption, courage, and generosity, and I have been blessed beyond words by many who have been trashed by this world and its inhabitants. I have passed on those blessings to my children and grandchildren, to colleagues, clients, diverse audiences, and the global church.

My journey into the world of trauma began with one victim of abuse who, in tiny increments, courageously shared her story with me. I asked questions and worked hard to listen carefully. I became her student and a student of many more—humans created by God, his own artwork, wounded and damaged. I sat with people and learned to say, in essence, "Teach me what it is like to be you." Somewhere along the way, the context of abuse broadened to include experiences at Christian camps, at schools, and in sports. I learned that boys and men were also abused.

I also worked with pastors, missionaries, and Christian leaders. They were depressed and anxious. They struggled with their roles and with the burdens of others. Many were burned out. And then one day everything collided as I began to realize that Christians in leadership positions were also abusing those under their care. This was difficult to absorb. I did not want it to be true. I didn't understand it. *I learned that what happens in families also happens in the family of God.*

Slowly, I began to understand that power, deception, and abuse were all tangled up together. People who were highly esteemed and seen as godly were in fact deceiving themselves and others in order to commit and conceal ungodly deeds. As time went on, I saw entire systems do the same thing. Systemic abuse, an utterly foreign concept to me at the time, became clearer as I discovered that sometimes the people of God unite to "protect" God's name by both committing and concealing actions that look nothing like God. God's people were breaking his heart.

I was angry. I wept. I wanted it not to be true, and I wanted to quit. Sometimes I felt as if I were swimming in a sewer with a sign above the entrance that read, "Sanctuary." I began to read everything I could to help me see. I went back to church history. I studied the Holocaust and other genocides. I read and reread the prophets, particularly Jeremiah. I buried myself in the Gospels. Little by little I began to see the systemic nature of abuse more clearly. I am still learning.

This book is the fruit of that process. God has invited us into the fellowship of his sufferings. It is not a place we want to go. It truly is a sewer. In entering, I began to learn that everything I encountered, Jesus had borne. That included my blindness, my resistance, and my fear of entering this place. But to refuse to enter, to turn away from what he sees, is to miss him. I have been given small glimpses into what it means to say, "The Word became flesh and lived among us" (John 1:14 NRSV). He was Immanuel in that space—God *with* us. And Christ calls us to be so like him in this world that others get a sense, a taste, of who he is and *know* that he is indeed with us.

I have been struck by how often we are told that Jesus *saw*. Matthew tells us that Jesus was going through all the cities and villages and that "*seeing* the people, He felt compassion for them, because they were distressed [harassed] and dispirited like sheep without a shepherd" (9:36 NASB). Jesus continues to see, and he invites us to stand with him and see—to feel the pain, the sorrow, the crushing, and the agony of precious sheep who have no shepherd, no caregiver, no comforter.

Much of Christendom today seems less interested in seeing as Jesus saw, less inclined to enter in, and far more interested in gaining power. We have acquired fame, money, status, reputation, and our own little kingdoms. We have read too many headlines about Christian leaders and Christian systems that look nothing like our Lord. I fear we have lost our way. It is time for those of us who name his name to stop and listen to our King, who was moved with compassion, a true Shepherd longing to both feed and enfold the sheep.

We follow a God who listens to us and weeps with us. That is evident in the life of Jesus. The incarnation is perhaps the greatest expression ever seen of empathic listening. Jesus came and pitched his tent among us—a virtual refugee camp. That meant drinking our water, sharing our chores, experiencing our losses, joining in our laughter, and weeping with us when we mourned. We need to learn to listen as he does. You see, he knows what it is like to be you. He has given you the gift of being heard and known and asks you, in turn, to give it to others. He longs for us to walk with him, caring for the distressed, the fleeced, the ones damaged by violence and tossed aside. He desires us to look with his eyes of love and hear with his keen ears. He has invited us to labor *with* him and to be with others just as he was.

It has been a great privilege for me to learn from our Shepherd. He has taken me to places I never imagined existed. I have seen evil, darkness, and despair in precious humans, God's artwork. I have certainly made many mistakes. However, I have found God present there, loving, teaching, carrying, and redeeming. I pray that as we look together at power and our often twisted and abusive manipulations of it, God's light will expose us. I pray that we will together bow before the One who sits on the throne and who bears scars that should be ours and that we will learn from the Good and Great Shepherd how to protect, feed, and be a refuge for the lambs he loves. It is not a pretty journey, but we will find him working with us as we go. Yes, he will use you to bless others. He will also use *them* to change *you* into a greater likeness of him. He always works both sides.

I pray that this book will increase awareness and understanding of power and its abuse so that we can protect and defend those who have been abandoned by Christianity's broken systems of power. For those who have been abused, my prayer is that in reading you will feel seen, protected, believed, and comforted. Some of you have left the church after experiencing abuses of power in the very place God means to be his sanctuary. If you see the church as a place of danger rather than of safety, please remember that, sadly, the church often fails to look and act like Jesus, making it easy to believe lies about who he is.

If you are a Christian leader, whether in a church, a nonprofit ministry, or another sphere of influence, I pray that you will come to understand the kinds of power—conscious and unconscious—that come with your authority. I pray that you will understand your own power and learn how to use it wisely—to bless and not to harm. If you have used power in a way that has inflicted harm, I pray that you will bow before the throne of the One who became small on our behalf and speak truth to yourself and to others about the damage you have done. May you desire the truth and grace of God more than the esteem of human beings.

I grieve that the body of Christ has so often walked away from this work and turned its back on Christ and his invitation. May we all learn how to discern when power is being used wrongly and call it by its right name. We have lost much and damaged many. We have broken God's heart. I pray that we will ardently seek after him in these matters. He waits.

PART 1

Power
Defined

one

The Source and Purpose
of Power

The dynamics of power are ever present in my Christian psychology practice. Power can be a source of blessing, but when it is abused, untold damage to the body and name of Christ, often *in* the name of Christ, is done. For the sake of that body and that wonderful name, I believe we need to wrestle with the issue of power and understand how it can be used for healing or harm, for good or evil. I invite you to look with me more closely at what power is, where it comes from, and the impact it has on all of us. Power is inherent in being human. Even the most vulnerable among us have power. How we use it or withhold it determines our impact on others.

Sarah is tiny and very frail, only four days old. She knows nothing about herself or the world in which she has landed. She has no words. She cannot effectively use her body to go anywhere. Something does not feel right. She doesn't know what is wrong, or why it is wrong, or how to tend to her own distress. Alone and in the dark, she cries. *And she has power.*

Two exhausted, sleeping adults, jolted from their comfortable bed and much-needed rest, quickly head toward the cry. She has disrupted two people who can use words, who know what they want as well as what she needs, and who can move their bodies as they choose. They understand the tiny one's cry and they respond, tossing aside how they feel, along with their preference for sleep. They choose to get up and comfort the little one and feed her with attention, love, and milk. In comparison to Sarah, these adults wield an astounding amount of power, and they choose to use their power to bless her with their care.

Our English word *power* (Latin: *posse*, meaning "be able") means "having the capacity to do something, to act or produce an effect, to influence people or events, or to have authority." It also has harsher meanings: to master, dominate, coerce, or force. By our sheer presence in this world, we, God's image bearers, have power. The four-day-old infant has the power to rouse independent grown-ups out of a greatly desired and much-needed sleep. The reverse is also true: those grown-ups have obvious power over the infant. They can respond with attention and care or with anger at being disturbed. They can withhold care and respond with neglect and silence. The infant influences the adults. The adult responses affect the child. The power of the vulnerable infant to express her needs exposes the hearts of the more powerful adults. Over time, their habituated response to the infant shapes not only the infant's personhood but also the hearts of the adults. Our responses to the vulnerable expose who we are. This is an important principle to keep in mind as we consider the use—and misuse—of power.

Anyone remotely in touch with today's news has some awareness of how power can be used for good and for evil. We read about authoritarian tyrants and about people being tortured and imprisoned for their faith or for criticizing their government. We also read about people who give sacrificially to those who need help, spending days to search for a lost child

4

or devoting time, money, and effort to rescue those trafficked by others. Both lists are endless. Every human life is a force in this world. Our influence pours out perpetually. But if those in authority refuse to help others, turn a deaf ear, and harden themselves to the needs of others, then rejection, not care, becomes the predominant influence.

Power in the Genesis Story

What is the source of our power as humans? In Genesis, we read about how God invested humans with power. "Then God said, 'Let Us make man in Our image, according to Our likeness; and let them rule over the fish of the sea and over the birds of the sky and over the cattle and over all the earth, and over every creeping thing that creeps on the earth.' God created man in His own image, in the image of God He created him; male and female He created them" (1:26–27 NASB). God made humans who bear his likeness and told them to rule. In Hebrew, the word *rule* means "to have dominion" or "to dominate." What did God tell them to rule over? Over the fish, the birds, the cattle, the whole earth, and every creeping thing. Note the stunning omission in God's directive: nowhere does he call humans to rule over each other! The man is not told to rule over the woman; neither is the woman to rule over the man. They are to rule together, in a duet, over all else God has created. They are to take the power God granted them and use it for good. Together. Genesis 1:28 continues with God telling humans to "fill the earth, and subdue *it*." *Subdue* means "to conquer," "to subjugate," or "to keep under." God created a one-flesh union and called that union of male and female to rule and subdue the earth, *not each other*.

Genesis 1 also tells us that God called Adam and Eve to fruitfulness. "God blessed them; and God said to them, 'Be fruitful and multiply'" (v. 28 NASB). How do we do that? Obviously, humans who are fruitful increase their power simply by creating more humans. But humans are also meant to be fruitful in all areas of life. In essence, God created us to multiply his image and likeness in everything we do. God created humans in his own image, in his likeness. Power was given to humans, who reflected the God who made them. And what do we know about this God? He is good; he is faithful; he is a refuge; he is truth; he is love. So, God gave human beings power in order that they might bear God's character in the world. And God blessed them; he pronounced a benediction over them and called them to be fruitful and multiply, to bear his likeness and bless the earth. Together.

We all know what happened after that. A cunning, deceptive creature who had utterly rejected the power of God and any likeness to him came and deceived the humans using God's own words. "You want to be like God? You want to be in his likeness? You want the ability to judge between good and evil? You can have that by choosing what he has denied you." And like the enemy, humans subsequently exercised their power to choose against God; they took what appeared good to them and fed themselves with it. The deception of promised good led them to choose disobedience to God. They used their power to choose evil when that power ought to have borne the likeness of God and been used to choose good. They wanted what they were meant to have: likeness to God. They wanted to discern good from evil. What they saw with their eyes appealed to their longings and their highest goal. But they took their God-given power and exercised it against him, deceived into believing they were choosing him.

They who bore the character of God used power in a way that gave them a likeness to the enemy of God. Like the king of Babylon, they said, "I will ascend above the tops of the clouds; I will *make myself* like the Most High" (Isa. 14:14 NIV). They forgot that any likeness to God was instilled by God himself.

6

Such a likeness cannot be humanly created. Their power was used not to bless but to harm, not just others but themselves as well. The abused power of the man and the woman produced outcomes that have rolled down from generation to generation, infecting us all.

Power of Personhood

To grasp the impact of power, we must have a sense of what a human is. Some concepts that have arisen out of my work with trauma victims may be helpful here.[1]

First, to be human is to have a voice. The voice of God spoke everything into existence. To be created in his image is to have a self, to have a voice and creative expression. Abuse of power silences that self and the words, feelings, thoughts, and choices of the victim. Their desires are disregarded and irrelevant. Abuse of any kind is always damaging to the image of God in humans. The self is shattered, fractured, and silenced and cannot speak who it is into the world.

Second, to be human is to be in relationship. We were created in relationship to God himself and to one another. God entered this world in the flesh to reestablish a relationship that was broken. His image is reflected in relationship. Humans long for safe relationship. Abusive power violates and shatters relationship. It brings betrayal, fear, humiliation, loss of dignity, and shame. It isolates, endangers, creates barriers, and destroys bonds. It destroys empathy, trashes safety, and severs connection. Abusive power has a profound impact on our relationship with God and with others. Victims of abuse often view God through a gravely distorted lens, seeing him as the source of the evil they experience. The violation and destruction of faith at times of tremendous suffering is one of the greatest tragedies of the abuse of power.

Third, to be human is to have power and to shape the world. As we have seen, our Creator called us to rule and subdue. Those are power words. Go have impact; go make things grow; go change things. Abuse quashes and removes power. A victim feels useless, powerless, and ineffective, and the loss of dignity and purpose is profound. We are meant to work, to make things happen, to make things change simply because we are here. These aspects of voice, relationship, and power are rooted in the character of God.

Types of Human Power

There are many types of power. Verbal power involves using words, often in artful ways, to manage situations and control others. Verbally gifted humans can use words to bless others or to do terrible, long-lasting damage. A related kind of power we rarely think about is silence. Silence can be a wonderful gift. Silence can also be a weapon. The sting of silence used to punish or ignore goes very deep.

Emotional power is often, though not always, paired with verbal power. Emotions can be used to comfort another with empathy or to control what people say and do, often intimidating and silencing them. The power of anger or rage can terrify a human being, with or without words.

Power can manifest itself in physical size or strength. If one person weighs 220 pounds and another weighs 85 pounds, the power differential is obvious. The bigger can easily injure or crush the smaller. Physical presence can be powerful in other ways too. We have all known someone who was not larger than everyone else but whose presence could fill a room. That power of personality can control a room, a company, and even a country.

People with specialized knowledge can wield great power, speaking authoritatively and expecting what they say to be accepted because they "know." Positions of authority confer power. If I am a president, a coach, a doctor, or a professor, my job gives me the right to say and do many things; the circle of my "ruling and subduing" is larger than most. Depending on my position and the way it is understood, I may use that power to justify many wrong things and overreach extensively, particularly if I'm a respected authority figure.

Like silence, absence also has great power. Do you remember playing the trust game as a child? Your friend stood behind you, and you were supposed to fall backward and trust that they would catch you. It was a bit scary. The absence of your friend, their failure to "show up," could mean injury. A parent who turns a blind eye to sexual abuse is absent when desperately needed. The result will be deep damage. The emotional absence of a spouse is deeply wounding. On the other hand, the refusal to join in with a group of bullies is a powerful and positive absence for the one being bullied.

Another type of power that some people wield is economic power. Money can buy many things in this world, and one of those things is power. That power can be used wisely and graciously—or it can be used to manipulate, control, and terrify.

Spiritual power is yet another kind of power that can be dangerous unless it is exercised in obedience to God. This form of power is used to control, manipulate, or intimidate others to meet one's own needs or the needs of a particular organization, often by using words cloaked in nice-sounding spiritual language and concepts.

Finally, our cultures, families, tribes, secular and religious communities, and nations all have tremendous power in shaping our minds and lives. Culture is like oxygen—it's always there, but we do not see it; it's simply what is. Experiencing a different culture of worship, food, or dress can be a shock. Culture can be wonderfully enriching. It can also be full of arrogance, prejudice, and division, so we must pay close attention and use our power and abilities to see and to think before swallowing the messages of our culture whole.

We will consider these kinds of power in much greater depth throughout this book. For now, we simply need to understand where power comes from and what its intended purpose is. We also need to be aware of the kinds of power we all have in varying degrees—and that we can use or withhold those powers for good or for evil. Finally, we need to see what it looks like when God-given power is used to bless.

Power Is Derivative

Two passages of Scripture will guide our understanding of a godly use of power. In Matthew 28:18–19, Jesus says, "*All* authority, *all* power is given to me; therefore go . . ."[2] Jesus holds all authority. That means any little bit of power you and I have is derivative; we are dispatched *under* his authority. Jesus does not give authority to us; he retains it. He is sending us out *under* his authority to carry out *his* enterprises in *his* way. Every drop of power you and I hold is shared power, given to us by the One who holds it all. It is not ours. It is his. He has shared what is rightfully his with us.

Are you verbally powerful? The Word gave you that power. Are you physically powerful? The mighty God, who breaks down strongholds and sustains the universe, gave you that power. Do you have a powerful position? It is from the King of Kings and the Lord of Lords. Do you have power of knowledge or skill? The Creator God, whose ways are beyond finding out, gave that power to you. Do you hold emotional power with others? That power came from the Comforter, the Wonderful Counselor. Do you have great financial power? If so, it is merely a small portion from the One who holds all riches. Any power that you and I hold is God's and has been given to us by him for the sole purpose of glorifying him and blessing others. If all power is derivative, then Christians should hold it with great humility. We are creatures, no more and no less. We follow the One who became flesh. Jesus models for us the humility of power.

In the second passage, we see that while Jesus was on earth, he said, "The Son can do nothing by himself; he can only do what he sees his Father doing" (John 5:19 NIV). The state of heart manifested by the Son of the Father should abound in those of us who follow him. We tout our own teachings, our own writings, our own organizations, and our own reputations. But Jesus did nothing of the sort. We seek a share of the glory and the power for ourselves. He humbled himself before both God and humans and became a servant. We seek to build our own little kingdoms. He came to build the Father's kingdom. God gives power to us as his creatures to be held in trust. Its purpose is to bless. If we understand the nature of power, both its source and its dangers, we will walk humbly before others, for our Master has said that if we would be chief, if we would lead and impact others, then we must serve. Before telling his disciples that he was sending them, Jesus said, "Look at my hands. Look at my feet" (Luke 24:39 NLT). These are the marks of his humility, the insignia of his authority, the visible evidence that he came to serve, not to be served. Those who follow him, endowed with his power, are called to go the way of the cross.

Power Comes from Our Hearts

Godly power starts in the kingdom of our hearts, is expressed in the flesh, and then moves out into the world. We make the mistake of seeing power as an external force. But power is *not* about having rule over a church, or a parishioner, or an institution, or a country. It's internal, not external. God's kingdom is the kingdom of the heart, not the kingdom of our churches, institutions, missions, or schools. God is building his kingdom, not ours, and he does that by exercising authority over the human heart to the extent that it is filled with the Spirit of Christ. *That* is godly power. And when we are full of God's power internally, we bring life and light and grace and truth and love into all our external enterprises, both great and small. God's kingdom grows, and he is glorified.

Any time we use power to damage or use a person in a way that dishonors God, we fail in our handling of the gift he has given. Any time we use power to feed or elevate ourselves, we fail in our care of the gift. Our power is to be governed by the Word of God and the Spirit of God. Any use that is not subject to the Word of God is a wrong use. Any use of power that is based on self-deception, when we have told ourselves that what God calls evil is instead good, is a wrong use. Remember, Adam and Eve, made in God's likeness, sought to be like him by eating what he had forbidden. The exercise of power in the choice to "be like" God required disobedience to God. It was therefore a wrong use of power. The exercise of the power of position to drive ministry workers into the ground "for the sake of the gospel" is also a wrong use of power. Using emotional and verbal power to achieve our own glory when God says he will share his glory with no one is a wrong use of power. The power of success or financial knowledge used to achieve ministry ends without integrity is a wrong use of power. Using theological knowledge to manipulate people to achieve our own ends is a wrong use of power. Exploiting our position in the home or the church to get our own way, serve our own ends, crush others, silence them, and frighten them is a wrong use of power. Using our influence or our reputation to get others to further our own ends is a wrong use of power.

Withholding power in the face of sin, abuse, and tyranny is also a wrong use of power. It is sin against God—complicity with the evil he hates. Jesus says, "Truly I tell you, whatever you *did not do* for one of the least of these, you *did not do* for me" (Matt. 25:45 NIV). Silence in the face of such evil can be a kind of abuse of power, for in staying silent about someone else's pain, we have nullified our God-given power to speak truth. God asks us to use our verbal power and to open our mouths for the mute, for those without such power. Complicity is a strangling of our God-given power meant to be active in this world on his behalf.

Godly power is derivative; it comes from a source outside us. It is *always* used under God's authority and in likeness to his character. It is *always* exercised in humility, in love to God. We use it first as his servants and then, like him, as servants to others. It is *always* used for the end goal of bringing glory to God. God is pleased with his Son. That means our uses of power must look like Christ because he is the One who brings God glory. So how will we serve? Here are three true stories that taught me lasting lessons about the beauty of power rightly used.

The first story takes place in a tiny fishing village in Brazil. A pastor there told me that *all*, not some, of the men in his village were alcoholics, batterers, and incestuous. "There are no exceptions, Diane—not the police, not the judge, and not the pastors." He asked me how he could help his people. I was initially speechless; his situation felt utterly hopeless. How does one shine light in such a place? And then I knew. I was standing with a man who carried the light of our God within. "I know it is overwhelming and feels hopeless," I responded, "but God put you here because you know him, and no one in this village has ever seen a life like yours with your family. They do not even know there is another way. Walk with Christ, honor your wife, bless your children, and God will illuminate his ways through you and awaken hunger in others for the way that you live." I didn't want to suggest in any way that the work God had put before him would be easy. Hoping to encourage him, I continued, "The task will be hard, sacrificial, and very slow, but there is hope. It is not in you. That hope is Christ in you in this dark place. By the power of God in your life, you can demonstrate, in the flesh, the life of a man who does not abuse power. As you drink deeply of Christ, from you will flow his living water, which will eventually change the landscape of the town."

The second story involves a conference for Arab women where we discussed trauma and its effects. Many of these women were victims of abusive power. At the end of my talk was a time for questions. One woman said this: "I was brought up in a Christian home. My father beat my mother and all his children horribly. Now I am married and have children. When we go to visit my parents and the children do something he does not like, my father beats them horribly. My husband and I do not believe that is of God, and we do not treat our children like that. Can you tell me what to do?"

Now, I am extremely cautious when I travel about sharing any negative thoughts I have regarding norms and practices in another culture. Even when asked direct questions, I'm careful in my responses. I asked this woman to give me a minute to think, because I knew if I spoke truth, it could result in violence against her. She and her family might be thrown out and disowned. I also knew that if I said nothing, I would encourage her to be complicit in the evil being done to her children—and she was clearly already convicted by God. And if I was silent, I would be complicit as well. So I paused momentarily to pray, and then I told her that I knew what I was about to say was difficult and potentially threatening to her. I agreed that her father was doing harm to her children, and it was not God's way. To speak truth to him, respectfully, was to use her power to bring God's light into the room, inviting her father to step into that light. To be silent was to teach her children that his behavior was right, rather than ungodly, and to model silence in the face of wrongdoing. It also meant being complicit in their harm. The room was very quiet. She was silent for a bit. Then she raised her head and said, "I will do what is right before God on one condition. I only ask that the women in this room commit to pray for me." They understood the monumental step she was taking and let her know they would be praying. I continue to do so.

The third story involves a man of great power. Some years ago, our son worked in the Middle East for a prince, a member of the royal household. My husband and I were invited as the prince's guests to see our son and visit the country.

We traveled on a fancy airline, with fancy seats and fancy food. Our son met us at the airport and whisked us away to the palace to meet the prince. I, a woman, would be walking into a room full of Arab men. I went over protocol carefully with our son. He instructed us to wait at the door to be greeted and not to speak first. The prince would remain seated. "Do not offer your hand," he said. "Do not sit until directed, and sit where you are told." To my son's knowledge, no other female had been in that room. He spent almost every evening there, so he knew.

We arrived and were escorted into the palace and taken to the meeting place. The room contained about fifteen Arab men in full regalia. My husband and I waited at the entrance. When instructed, we walked in. No sooner had we done so than the prince stood, walked quickly over to us, and warmly extended his hand to me. He greeted me by name, introduced himself by his first name, and showed me to the seat at his right hand. All fifteen men followed his example. They did what their prince did. We were greatly honored and graciously welcomed.

This man would have been well within his rights to follow protocol. In fact, he risked criticism and the loss of respect for breaking the social rules. But he chose to gather up his power and use it to pour out blessing—which is what he continued to do the entire time we were there. He illustrates what a person of much power looks like when they do not clutch glory but rather seek to use that power to bless others.

These stories help us imagine how God would have us exercise our power. I believe that God would have us use our power as benediction, to bless, by way of sacrifice, by way of the cross.

The Brazilian pastor living sacrificially in that seacoast town—one man, one family, full of the light of the love of Christ, illuminating a very dark world—embodies in his life what Jesus did in his own life. The King of Kings became one man, finite, living in time and place. He was full of light and love, ministering one by one and always faithful to the Father.

The lovely Arab woman living sacrificially—bringing light and love by speaking truth to power, refusing complicity with evil done in the name of God—blesses her father with a firm but respectful invitation to the light. She blesses her children, for they will see and know a new way and come to understand that culture, even so-called Christian culture, often fails to follow Christ. She will look like Jesus, who spoke truth to the religious leaders and confronted those who crushed the little ones.

And the gracious sheikh who, for love of our son, blessed my husband and me—stepping across all those divides that protect his name and status, inviting us to sit at his right hand and be waited on and receive honor from the one we came to honor—gave us a small but rich taste of the Lord of heaven and earth seated on the throne. This earthly prince, who inspired awe in me by crossing over position, tradition, culture, gender, and training to greet me with his right hand, reminds me of the awe due to my true Lord, who at a cost beyond measure crosses over the barriers of highest position and of sin and death to welcome me at the right hand of the Father.

It is my prayer, as we think together about the power bestowed on us by God, that we will let his light shine in as we study and listen well. May we, his children, see clearly the truth about earthly power and not be seduced. May we not deceive ourselves or others regarding any use of power that is not under the authority of the One who holds all power. May we live in dark places, shining the light of Christ on the abuses around us, even when they are in our own circles. May we speak to those who are crushing God's little ones or robbing the people in his churches. And may we, like our Lord, lay aside every bit of earthly power to cross divides, step out of high positions, and reach out with love to those who are vulnerable, whose power is little or trampled, bestowing benedictions as we go.

two

Vulnerability and Power

We are frail, finite creatures. Whether one sits on the throne of the Roman Empire or in the papal seat, whether one leads a lucrative organization or pastors a megachurch, whether one is an undocumented immigrant or a newborn babe, all are vulnerable, all the time. There are no exceptions. To be vulnerable is to have the capacity to be wounded. Just as power can harm or bless, vulnerability leaves humans open to being blessed and hurt, to good and evil. Vulnerability and power are intertwined, engaged in a dance that is sometimes beautiful and sometimes destructive. This complex relationship is poorly understood and seldom discussed.

Remember our newborn girl? She is the essence of vulnerability. She can do nothing for herself and is utterly dependent on adults who care for her. How they use their power not only impacts her but tells us something about them. If they value this little one, then even when their own needs are not being met or their preferences honored, she will be protected and safe, nurtured and loved. If they do not care for her or if they exploit her vulnerability, she will either die or grow up bent in unhealthy ways. Their use of power determines whether she will live or die and how she will grow. It is not hard for us to grasp the vulnerability of the newborn.

The dynamics are complicated, though. Suppose our newborn, Sarah, was the first child of a sixteen-year-old girl who grew up without good parenting and has no idea who her father is. Sarah lived with her mother, who abused drugs, in a violent neighborhood. There were many men coming in and out of her home. In fact, Sarah is the child of one of those men, a child of rape. If we go back to her mother's story, we will find an extended history of vulnerability exploited rather than protected—generations of people who needed safety and care and never received it, generations of humans creating others in their likeness, not just physically but in many other ways. Though they are created in the image of God, that image has never been nurtured by someone who cares for them in the way God does. When God's image is thus clouded, it's easy for us to treat such people as "less than." They know only two ways to use power: to protect themselves (because they are vulnerable) and to exploit others (because they are vulnerable). Often exploitation can seem like self-protection.

In Sarah's situation, the vulnerability is screamingly obvious, but that's not always the case. John is a multimillionaire, educated at a prestigious school, married with two children, and CEO of a large company. He has a tremendous amount of power over many lives. But deep inside lurks a vulnerability he works hard to hide, even from himself. You see, John grew up with a very wealthy father who was rarely present, physically or emotionally. This father frequently humiliated John and his brother, attacking their capabilities, characters, accomplishments, and appearances. John's mother was quiet and fearful, always looking for ways to appease her husband. So these children marinated in the exploitation and abuse of their vulnerability rather than experiencing safety within it. They too were unprotected.

John's response to this abuse is to pursue power and protect himself against vulnerability. His fear of vulnerability leads him to humiliate, condemn, and control women. He does this to employees and to his wife and daughter. He also has a secret life visiting sex workers, whom he treats with loathing and rage. He does not understand why he cannot stop these behaviors. John is vulnerable and damaged, and he copes by seeking power, abusing it, and in turn damaging vulnerable people in his world.

We often think of vulnerability as "weakness," as if there is something flawed about the person who is vulnerable. But we are all obviously physically vulnerable. No matter how much power we have, we will inevitably die. Most of us will deal with a sickness or two before we go. People who led great armies and who were greatly feared are dead. Eventually, something overcame them. You will never, by intelligence, accomplishment, seat of power, respect, or any other thing, be able to make yourself invulnerable. Welcome to the human race.

But vulnerability is also a gift. Being susceptible to the many dangers in our fallen world is not something we desire. But if we take no risks, we miss out on many wondrous aspects of God's world. As a young girl, I loved to ice skate. But I never would have enjoyed the wonderful and exhilarating experience of moving across the ice if I had not been willing to fall. I loved to climb trees . . . up high and again vulnerable to harm. Had I not taken these risks, I would have closed myself off to activities that brought joy.

To be receptive to the love of another and to give love in return is to risk injury and rejection. When you offer love to another human being, you expose yourself to the possibility of betrayal. Ask any parent who is suffering with a beloved child gone astray. But a failure to love because it renders you vulnerable will rob you of laughter, companionship, accomplishments together, and oneness of heart. The love between good friends is a thing of beauty and wonder. It's also risky because it increases your capacity for being wounded. In fact, the more people you love, the more vulnerable to wounding you become. Even if all those relationships go well, some people you love will likely die before you do, and your vulnerability will result in great grief.

To marry is to be vulnerable to abandonment, betrayal, and criticism from the one to whom you gave yourself. To bear children is to be vulnerable, for they may bring you great joy or crushing sadness. To speak publicly, to teach, to lead—all these things open us to criticism or failure. To care for sick patients is to be vulnerable, for you might become sick yourself. You may be a brilliant and accomplished doctor, but if you treat COVID-19, you make yourself very vulnerable.

Many of us work hard to *not* be vulnerable. Yet we are wise to see our vulnerability as a welcome gift, albeit one that needs to be guarded and not exposed indiscriminately. We won't always have a choice, since those who violate and exploit do not usually ask for permission. But if we fail to acknowledge our vulnerability, then we limit our ability to choose well when we are able to choose. If the person driving you home has been drinking, you choose not to make yourself vulnerable to their drunk driving by finding another ride home. If you need surgery, you do not put yourself under the knife of a gang leader. You seek out the best surgeon possible. If there is a bully in the neighborhood, you work hard to protect your children and others from his bullying and do what you can to stop it.

There are many situations in life in which exposing our vulnerability is unwise. Many people are not aware of that. If you grow up never having experienced a safe relationship, then your capacity for judging safety is highly compromised. How will you recognize something you have never seen? That lack of understanding can lead to years of abusive relationships, or generations of them, because vulnerability has never been understood, protected, and valued. Each new relationship carries hope that *this* person will feed your hungry soul, but without the knowledge required to read the signs, you may be looking at the next wolf and fail to perceive that it's time to run.

The truth is that vulnerability is always there. We can use discernment about what to do when it's exposed, some of the time; we can protect ourselves and others when it is wise to do so, if we are able. We can also be aware of the vulnerabilities of others and walk softly in their presence. But to live or love or have compassion is to risk harm, exploitation, and betrayal. Avoidance of living or loving won't protect us, certainly not from death, but it will certainly ensure that we live a hungry life, not to mention we will look nothing like our Lord, who became vulnerable on our behalf.

Vulnerability and Exploitation

Our capacity for being wounded is a constant. Sadly, oftentimes our collective response when someone is wounded is to blame them. If they had not done _____ (action), then maybe _____ (consequence) would not have happened.

A female college student decides to go out on the weekend with two friends. They go to the local "in" spot where many students congregate. She has a drink, then orders several more. Clearly intoxicated, she gets up to leave but can't walk steadily. She is in danger of falling or passing out. Another student comes over and says he will walk her back to her dorm room. She's vulnerable.

Two different scenarios could emerge. The student could assist her back to her dorm, carefully making sure she doesn't fall or step out into the street, and notify someone at her residence about her condition and her need for care. Or he could walk her out of the restaurant, take her to a solitary spot, rape her, and leave her there. When she finally came out of her alcohol haze, she would find herself disheveled, exposed, and lying on the ground alone.

What kind of response do we have to these scenarios? In the first place, we are likely to think that the young woman was unwise to risk hurting herself or being hurt by another. She made herself extremely vulnerable, most likely without considering the possible consequences. Those assessments would be accurate. She ratcheted up her level of vulnerability and left herself unguarded and exposed to harm on many levels. There may be reasons, unknown to us, behind her drinking that night that would elicit empathy, rather than judgment, for the pain she was medicating. Suppose she had just returned to school after burying her mother. We would understand her pain.

In the first ending to this story, we note that the young man's assistance in getting her to safety was kind and thoughtful. Where she had left herself unwisely vulnerable, he stepped in and protected her. We would find his actions honorable. His actions toward her tell us about his character. He exercised power over her vulnerability and revealed himself to be safe, kind, and responsible.

The second scenario may elicit different responses. Many will assume that if the young woman had not gotten drunk, she would not have been raped. Some will go so far as to suggest that "boys will be boys," saying she should have known better than to put herself in a position in which a young man clearly couldn't help himself. Or some may even imply that sex is what she wanted in the first place and that now she wants to deny her desire by calling it rape. Such responses present us with a significant problem: they are antithetical to Scripture. Remember our newborn? Her vulnerability exposes the hearts of her caregivers.

Many years ago, I taught a seminary class on clergy sexual abuse. At one point in the lecture I said, "As pastors, you will have power in your relationships with congregants . . . always.

Whether you feel powerful or vulnerable, at any given time, you're the one with the power in that relationship. Your words and actions carry authority. If a woman comes to see you for counseling about her marriage and one day, confused and longing for attention, she stands up and undresses in front of you, *what happens next depends entirely on you.* What she has done tells us some things about her, for sure. But what you do in response tells us about you. It tells us what you are like in the presence of unfettered vulnerability." The classroom was very quiet.

The exploitation of the vulnerable person tells us about the exploiter, not the victim of that exploitation. How can I say that with such certainty? Listen to the Word of God: "What comes *out* of a person is what defiles him. For *from within*, out of the heart of man, come evil thoughts, sexual immorality, theft, murder, adultery, coveting, wickedness, deceit, sensuality, envy, slander, pride, foolishness. *All these evil things come from within*, and they defile a person" (Mark 7:20–23 ESV). In essence, Mark is saying that what comes out of a person exposes the heart *of that person.* "To defile" is to make unclean, to pollute, or to make profane (render ourselves ungodly). We pollute ourselves by our own thoughts, words, and deeds. To put it bluntly, we soil ourselves.

And then, of course, we reach for deception in order to reframe, rename, and protect ourselves. We say, "I did not do it; it was someone else's fault." We deceive ourselves and in turn work to deceive others. The young man in the second scenario will do this regarding his exploitation of the young woman. "I had sex with her because she . . ." If the rape is reported, he may have friends and family who will support his view. Wrong choices and inaccurate labeling of exploitations of another's vulnerability cause further damage to ourselves and others. But the truth is that our response to vulnerability tells about us and only us. What comes "out of us" in the face of vulnerability

25

was there all the time. The vulnerability of the other has merely exposed the truth about ourselves.

Here the story line should sound familiar. Adam and Eve were created in the likeness of God and given power for the purpose of blessing. They were also given a choice between trusting God as preeminent or relying on their own thoughts and desires. Given that choice, we see that even in a perfect world, humans were vulnerable, susceptible to choosing "not God." God did not create automatons; God wanted flesh-and-blood humans who could *choose* to love. The capacity to love makes everyone vulnerable . . . even God. By creating us in such a fashion, he opened himself up to failure and injury. And injured he has been! God's words were twisted by the deceiver, and his beloved creatures chose to step into that deception. What followed was more deception and blame.

Like our first parents, we also have choices about our own vulnerability. Some of us are not aware of that fact yet, which renders us even more vulnerable. Some are determined to see themselves as an unassailable fortress, which is also dangerous. Others have never known protection and safety and have never learned how to make wise choices regarding their vulnerability. As we struggle, eventually we need to realize that our vulnerability is part of being human. We also need to recognize that we can make choices to serve ourselves or make them under the governance of our God. If we disregard him, we will surely fail to protect ourselves and others wisely; we will use our power in wrong ways. And in any debacle we create for ourselves or others, we will likely respond with deception and blame.

Any time we confront vulnerability in a newborn, a confused teen, a person hungry for love and attention and looking in all the wrong places, or a sick or weak or impaired person, what comes out of us tells us about us. Are we compassionate? Protective? Or are we exploitive, feeding off the vulnerable to meet our own needs?

Jesus Becomes Vulnerable for Us

Jesus has led the way in teaching us about vulnerability, deception, and power. In Philippians 2:7, we are told that Jesus came in the likeness of a man. How do humans come? They come like our little newborn girl. When he who holds all power came as one who had no power, he laid aside what he was, and he assumed what he was not. He wore our vulnerability in his flesh. "You will find a baby wrapped in swaddling clothes and lying in a manger" (Luke 2:12 ESV). Jesus entered into our vulnerability. He who clothed the universe had to be fed and clothed. His family had to flee as refugees on his behalf. He had to eat, work, learn, and relate. He had to learn how to navigate hatred, fear, criticism, and rejection. He also had to make choices to protect himself. In Luke 4, we read that the people drove Jesus out of the city, led him to a precipice, and tried to throw him off. He somehow passed through the middle of the crowd and escaped. He protected himself; he made the choice to do so. It is important that we recognize that protecting ourselves when we are vulnerable is not wrong.

Jesus also protected others when they were vulnerable. In John 8, a woman caught in adultery was dragged by religious leaders and dropped in front of Jesus to test him. (Interestingly, they "forgot" to bring the man!) The religious leaders said that Moses had commanded that such a person be stoned. What Moses actually said in Deuteronomy 22:24 is that both parties should be stoned. The leaders were not following their own Scriptures. The woman was in a vulnerable situation, and in response, Jesus protected her.

Jesus took on vulnerability when he became human. We can't have one without the other. We also know that in the end he did not protect himself at all. He gave himself to the devouring wolves who viciously abused their power to crush him. He did so for our sakes. He had a choice to protect himself at every juncture. Jesus said, "My kingdom is not of this world. If my kingdom were of this world, my servants would have been fighting, that I might not be delivered over to the Jews. But my kingdom is not from the world" (John 18:36 ESV). Why did he do this? Why did he fail to draw on power that was rightly his? Having taken on our vulnerability, he rescued us from our own self-destruction. Why? "I always do what pleases [the Father]" (8:29 NIV). He did what Adam and Eve failed to do. They bowed to deception and did what seemed pleasing to themselves. Jesus bowed to the Father and did what was pleasing to him. He obeyed the law: love God with everything you are and have; make that love preeminent over all else no matter what. That was ever and always behind his actions. That is why he protected himself. That is why he protected others. And that is why he has protected us eternally.

You and I struggle to understand our own vulnerabilities and to manage them wisely. We struggle not to blame circumstances or other people when our hearts are exposed. We struggle to understand our relationships with others and their vulnerabilities. We struggle to know how we might respond or where we are in danger of exploiting them. May we struggle as those who carry the likeness of God in us, always doing what pleases the Father. There is no formula. We will often err. But we follow the One who became like us so that we might become like him, vulnerable children of the Most High God, who became vulnerable for us.

three

The Role of Deception
in the Abuse of Power

How is it that humans are so easily led to misuse power? Power was given to us so we could do good, yet why do we so often use it for evil instead? Deception seems to be a key factor in leading us to use power to take what is not ours and that which will bring death. Any study of power misused is also always a study of deception, first of the self and then of others.

Let's return to that first deception. Genesis 3:1 says that "the serpent was more crafty, sly, or shrewd than any beast . . . that the LORD had made." The deceiver asked Eve, "Has God *really* said you shall not eat of every tree in the garden?" He altered what God had said and took God's word beyond the boundaries God had set. Eve grasped the first deception. "No," she said. "We can eat from the trees—except for one." But she went on to say, "If we even touch the one in the middle, we will die" (vv. 2–3). Note that God had said *nothing* about touching the tree. Eve herself twisted God's words even as she attempted to correct the serpent's deception.

The master deceiver told her she would not die, as if somehow that was not what God had meant. Surely she must have misunderstood him. He really meant that if you eat, your eyes will open, and you will be like God, knowing good *and evil*. God created humans in his image, which was a glorious thing. But in *not knowing evil*, they were unlike him. He protected the vulnerable, those who were not equipped to know evil and remain undamaged by it. He also created a choice for them. God pointed out a toxin in the midst of abundant good and invited them to choose him over everything else. That invitation was the choice to repeatedly bend themselves toward God. Such a bending would shape them, strengthen them, and increase their likeness to him. Eve was seduced by this argument and chose to believe the serpent's variation of God's words rather than God himself. She took in what she thought was good and beautiful and would give her wisdom. She believed the variation given by someone other than God and made a judgment based on external appearances and was thereby deceived and damaged. She ingested the toxin and bent herself away from the God who loved her.

We too deceive ourselves, ingesting what is toxic and labeling what we're doing as good for, or even protective of, his church. John, the beloved of Christ, wrote a letter toward the end of the first century because believers were being deceived. He wrote to them about light and darkness, truth and error, righteousness and lawlessness, life and death. In 1 John 1:5–10 he tells us that we can be sure we know God *if we obey him*. We can say we love him, but if we hate another or judge them as "less than," we are liars. We can say we love him, but if we bend ourselves toward something other than God to satisfy our hunger, we ingest toxins into our souls. We can say we love God, but if we deem victims of abuse or people of another race or ethnicity as less than, we make it clear that we are liars and the truth is not in us. We are deceived.

John goes on to say that we are not to love the world or the things in the world. We are not to give ourselves away to achieving success measured by earthly outcomes, even in the church. We are to be governed by love and obedience to Jesus Christ no matter the outcome. John mentions longings for material things such as wealth, buildings, and numbers. He talks about the longing for what we see or envision down the road, for the tangible. Last, he mentions the pride we have in our achievements or positions. John says that the love of status and earthly externals is an indicator that the love of the Father does not dwell in us. These are the things by which we are so easily seduced, even in Christendom.

As God's people, we are susceptible to being deceived by what we see, what we long for, and what we name good. We are too generous in our self-trust—willing to give ourselves the benefit of the doubt. We start by labeling things inaccurately. Eve did it. When asked about the tree, she said that if they ate from it *or touched it*, they would surely die. God had said nothing about touching the tree. In that statement, she had already abandoned truth for deception. She had taken what God said and added to it. We often misname things by adding what God never intended.

We distort God's Word by adding to it. We say that love of God requires this list of rules and that if you do not follow them, you are disobedient to God. Jesus spoke harshly with the Pharisees for doing exactly that. "They bind heavy burdens, hard to bear, and lay them on men's shoulders" (Matt. 23:4 NKJV). We tell victims of atrocious, life-altering abuse to simply forgive and forget. Forgiveness of any wrong, let alone a life-shattering one, is never a "just do it" task. Nor do our minds forget. Hopefully time and hard work, and some level of healing, may change our relationship with those memories. But forget? Who forgets being raped or having their bones crushed by the one they call husband or being trafficked by the one they call Daddy? It is easy to misrepresent God's truth to ourselves and to others. Eve did so to herself, and then she went on to share her deception with Adam, and he also deceived himself. We convince ourselves, and sometimes others, that we are doing good when we are not. We bring them into our deceptions. We feel validated in our choices by doing so. But there was a significant voice missing in these choices. The prophet Jeremiah quotes God as saying, "Through their deceit they refuse to know Me" (Jer. 9:6 NASB). Is that not exactly what Adam and Eve did—ignored the voice of God? Is that not what we do?

We sanction millions of dollars being used fraudulently "for God" with no concern for those we are lying to. We tolerate bullying at the helm of a "Christian" organization because "that is just the way he is." We protect a gifted youth leader because the numbers are growing, even though several have come forward and haltingly spoken of abuse. We tell boys and girls that the pastor or coach or leader in the church family could not possibly have meant anything sexual. In overlooking the toxins, we, like the Israelites, refuse to acknowledge God. Rather than seeking God's voice when feeling the pull into deception, we accept being deceived for the sake of a "good" cause with God's name attached.

Jeremiah said, "The heart is more deceitful than all else and is desperately sick; who can understand it?" (17:9 NASB). If the full force of this statement hit us, we would be afraid to get out of bed. The Hebrew word for deceit includes meanings such as "insidious," "sly," and "slippery." I was struck by such definitions following a trip to Rwanda. The levels of deception and the gross misuse of power in any genocide are shocking. But in this case, the church in Rwanda was grievously complicit in the genocide that claimed the lives of some eight hundred thousand people. The church wanted purity. But pursuit of that kind of "purity" meant flagrant, hateful disobedience to God. The church bought the deception that some Rwandans were impure and thus needed to be eradicated. Deception led those who called themselves God's people to crush, dehumanize, and destroy humans created in God's likeness. They had been called by God to be a light in their world and to expose the deeds of darkness. Instead, they melted into that darkness and used Scripture to "sanctify" it.

The Process of Deception

Though the fruit of deception can be quite apparent, deception is by its nature often difficult to see. We experience this when someone we revere is exposed for years of sexual abuse or fraud. We thought we were looking at an honest, good person. We did not see the marks on the trail of detectable evidence. How does such a thing develop, and why is it so difficult to see? And when it is exposed, why are we so determined to deny the truth and thus deceive ourselves?

Deception starts with the self, not others. This was true of Satan. He deceived himself into thinking he could and should be like the Most High. He now works to deceive us, and our own deceptive hearts are ready to partner with him in this endeavor. We find ways to tell ourselves things that are not true so we can believe them and act on them without internal conflict. I need to get a good grade on this test. If I don't, I'll fail the test and the course. I cannot fail because my parents have sacrificed for me to come to this school. They will be angry and ashamed of me. I'll cheat just this once *for the sake of my parents.* That line of thinking is a replica of what happened in the garden. I will do this thing for a good purpose; therefore, it is good. I will eat this fruit so I can have God's likeness. God wants me to have his likeness. I have convinced myself, by way of deception, that wrongdoing is right. I have numbed any feelings of fear or guilt by deceiving myself and calling evil good.

The most effective lies are those that contain some truth. I've worked with people for many years, and I've seen this pattern play out repeatedly. People inoculate themselves with a good thought so they can justify the wrongdoing they are about to choose—a common mechanism among fallen human beings.

Think about this description of deception in connection to situations in your own world involving sexual abuse, domestic violence, embezzling of funds, infidelity, and various addictions. Also consider that when a person feeds on affirmation or success—or demands that others agree with them—similar deceptions are involved, though these may be less overt behaviors. Temptation arises, self-deception or delusion joins in, evil is called good or is at least justified, and over time the choice is habituated and the prisoner is trapped, actively participating and barreling toward death. Every time we call a lie the truth, we damage our capacity to make moral judgments. "To some extent, I find sin like coffee," says a character in Joe R. Lansdale's *The Thicket*. "When I was young and had my first taste of it, I found it bitter and nasty, but later on I learned to like it by pouring a little milk in it, and then I learned to like it black. Sin is like that. You sweeten it a little with lies, and then you get so you can take it straight."[1]

When laid out like this, deception sounds repellent, even horrifying. But it shows up in our ministries and in our lives in subtle ways, sometimes even in pretty packages. Deception can easily lie below the surface of a high position, great theological knowledge, stunning verbal skills, and excellent performance. As a matter of fact, those are power tools that allow people to live deceptively *and* to hide the fact that they are doing so. Those external factors become a motive for deception. If the enemy of our souls can appear as an angel of light, then surely an evil human being, who is in fact mimicking him, can appear well clothed, theologically articulate, and beautiful to the human eye.

As I wrote in a previous book, *Suffering and the Heart of God*, "Self-deception functions as a narcotic in protecting us from seeing or feeling that which is painful to us."[2] A narcotic that reduces pain is easily abused. Over time, our ability to carry pain, work with it, or find healthy ways of ameliorating it decreases, and we increasingly depend on the narcotic to cope. The opioid crisis in the United States is a startling illustration of these dynamics. Like opioids, deceptions block pain, help us relax, and help us calm down because, by way of deception, we have "fixed" what was distressing. In addition, we get good at what we practice. The more we practice something, the more we're able to do it without conscious thought. It becomes habituated, and we can do it while thinking of other things. That works great for tying shoes. It's terrifying when it comes to deceiving ourselves and others.

Jeremiah has essentially told us that our deception deceives us. As with a physical narcotic, the more repeatedly we use deception, the weaker our ability to resist. Again and again, our judgment is twisted by lies until deception is a habit and the power to recognize and choose what is good dies. That is what's at play for someone who has sexually abused children. If they ever had any torment regarding their actions, it's long since dead. Howard Thurman says it this way: "The penalty of deception is to *become* a deception, with all sense of moral discrimination vitiated. A man who lies habitually becomes a lie, and it is increasingly impossible for him to know when he is lying and when he is not."[3]

Deception is also contagious; it was transmitted from the enemy to Eve, to Adam, to us. We are invested in believing things said by those who matter—a child, a spouse, a pastor. We might learn that a well-loved church leader has been sexually abusing multiple women in the church. No one wants that to be true, so we jump to his defense, desperate to prove the accusers false. The deception becomes groupthink. We use our collective power to circle the wagons and to protect what we desire to be true. The deception grows to envelop many people who have corporately injected the narcotic rather than face the destruction and the pain that will accompany the truth. Deception has now become systemic.

The Damaging Power of Deceit

Deceiving ourselves and others always leads to death. Listen to these words from noted writer and Auschwitz survivor Elie Wiesel: "I pinched myself. Was I still alive? Was I awake? How is it possible that men, women, and children were being burned and that the world kept silent? No. All this could not be real, a nightmare, perhaps. Soon, I would wake up with a start. . . . I told my father that I could not believe that human beings were being burned in our times. The world would never tolerate such crimes. 'The world,' he said, 'the world is not interested in us. Today, everything is possible, even the crematoria.'"[4]

"Everything is possible," said the father to his fifteen-year-old son as they sat in a concentration camp. It was indeed possible for human beings to burn children and vulnerable adults and for no one to help. You see, if we look further back, we find in Jeremiah and other places that the Israelites sacrificed their children to the fire. Why? To appease God, to stay in his good graces. They sacrificed their children to the Canaanite god Moloch. In their twisted thinking, they did what the God of Israel forbade them to do in order to earn his favor, to please him. The Nazis were not the first to burn children. God's people did so long before.

I have stood in Auschwitz beside those ovens where children and other vulnerable people were thrown. And why were they thrown there? For the sake of "purity." For us to be pure, we must get rid of certain kinds of humans; we must silence them, eliminate them, because they are a threat to our purity and our prosperity. A staggering deception! Yet is that not what we do when we cast truth-telling victims of abuse from our midst and label them "disruptive"? Is that not what we do when we divorce ourselves from another ethnic group, deeming them unlike "us"? We throw "them" in the ovens of shame, less than, isolation, liars, dirty, and many other labels.

I have been to Rwanda, where those who were called cockroaches needed to be destroyed so the people could be "purified." As if people could be purified by slaughtering precious souls God himself had made. And have we not done the same with the machine of slavery, lynching, beating, isolation, and humiliation? Have we not done it with Indigenous peoples, whom we've labeled dirty and put behind fences? Any group of people that names the name of Christ and does such things creates a place of death.

Contemplate the church's many deceptions regarding those seen as less than in various ways. As we will see, deceptions are systemic, meaning entire human systems perpetrate lies as truth. We believe our denomination or our church has the only correct doctrine. We believe our race is superior and needs to be protected above others at all costs. We believe only one gender, one race, one group is capable of holding power. We are right and everyone else is somehow substandard. Virulent deceptions that destroy lives and entire nations are clung to as truth. If you doubt this, hang out on "Christian" social media for a week.

We see an example of systematic deception in the way the church has bought into lies about race and is not even yet aware of the depth of those deceptions and their ongoing damage. We have utterly deceived ourselves into thinking that separateness from others who are in some way unlike us is good. And the people of God, whom he will one day unite, have yet to see the damage done to those who were battered and enslaved in God's name and how that damage is still running down through the generations.

Another place the church is involved in systematic deception is in our unwillingness to stand up for the victims of abusive power. The *Houston Chronicle* exposed systemic deception in the Southern Baptist Convention regarding decades of ignoring and hiding countless acts of sexual abuse and rape and protecting the perpetrators.[5] Those deceptions are still being uncovered. The damage to victims is immeasurable. There is harm done to us as well because any time we deceive ourselves, we do damage to our lives and our souls. All these things were carried out using God's house and God's Word to sanction the deceptions, the behaviors, and the cover-up of evils.

Every time we deceive ourselves into thinking that what God calls evil is in fact good, something dies. With slavery, those in power killed many human beings, along with things such as dignity, choice, flourishing, voice, and love. The act or cover-up of abuse kills as well. It kills hope, trust, safety, dignity, and love. G. Campbell Morgan says this: "Sanctuary means having no complicity with anything that makes sanctuary a necessity."[6] The church and the individuals in it have been complicit with horrific things that call for sanctuary. We are called to be a sacred place for the vulnerable. We have often chosen to be a safe place for the powerful and have deceived ourselves into believing that God would call that good.

Not only is deception contagious and systemic, but it is easily passed down through the generations. This means that the church's failure both crushes present victims and harms generations to come. The church, God's instrument, which was meant to use its power to pour out blessing through the ages, becomes a machine for deceptions that are passed on again and again.

Personal and social identity are formed during the developmental years by parents and extended family, those with power in a child's life. Those identities can be lies. A little girl can grow up utterly deceived about what it means to be female. She may learn that females are trash, sexual objects to be used on a whim, or stupid. If she voices a thought, she will be humiliated. Or she may learn that she is precious and that she is to be nurtured well and safely so she can learn and grow and become the woman God means her to be. Her mind is developed; she learns strength and is encouraged to have a voice. Likewise, a little boy can grow up nurtured and loved. He can be taught kindness and shown that strength of any kind is to be used to bless others. Or he can be taught that he has power to use for whatever suits him, that rage is an interpersonal skill, and that he should do whatever it takes to get what he wants. The abuse of women and children, hatred and violence toward other ethnic groups, condemnation of all who believe differently, and many other lies are often passed down through the generations. Deceptions that God hates become beliefs tightly held and treated like a rock on which to stand. Humans find sanctuary in lies rather than in God himself, the God of truth and light.

The Way of Truth

Here is truth: John tells us in his first epistle that "those who do not love abide in death. Everyone who hates their brother or sister is a murderer. . . . Whoever sees their brother or sister in need and closes their heart against him or her, how does the love of God abide in them? Let us not love with word or tongue, but with deed and truth" (1 John 3:14–15, 17–18). In the beginning, God said, "If you eat of that one tree, you will die" (Gen. 2:17). He spoke truth. Adam and Eve distorted God's words, and death came. Now God has said, "If you hate, death will come to you." So many of our deceptions exist to feed our desires and protect ourselves without regard for others and our impact on them.

The Greek word for "hate" in this verse means "to kill," but it can also mean "to spit on someone in your heart." It means "to tear down or destroy another," and John says we can do that simply by closing our hearts against those in need. Deceived hearts are closed hearts. They are closed first to the God of truth and second to other humans. Deception *always* does damage to the one deceiving and to those being deceived. When we close our hearts, we have in essence spit on people in our hearts. John pleads with us not to love just with words. We can be quite good at loving in that way and can deceive ourselves that it is sufficient. But we are to love in action and in truth. That means we are to match God's standard of both love and truth. It means we will not deceive ourselves or others and will be people of truth all the way through. In other words, we will have integrity, the opposite of deception. The word *integrity* comes from *integer*, which means "whole." It refers to something that is the same all the way through.

John says to the people of God, "Do not capitalize on talking" (which is very often our vehicle for deception); "instead, love with deed" (the word *deed* implies hard labor, hard work) "and love with truth, without deception" (1 John 3:18). What John is describing is using power to bless. Loving by our actions and with truth means our lives will be a blessing to those around us. Deception is the antithesis of love. When we deceive, it is obviously the antithesis of truth. We have not spoken truth to ourselves, nor have we given it to others. The fruit of deception is damage to the self and then to others such as our families, churches, and nations. God said we shall surely die if we eat that fruit.

Listen to Jeremiah again:

> I weep day and night
>   for the slain of the daughter of my people.
> . . . .

> They have bent their tongues for lies.
>> They are not valiant for the truth on the earth.
> . . . .
> Everyone will deceive his neighbor
>> and will not seek the truth;
> they have taught their tongue to speak lies
> . . . Your dwelling place is in the midst of deceit;
>> through deceit they refuse to know me, says the
>> LORD. (Jer. 9:1, 3, 5–6)

Deception of any kind or size brings death. It has been so from the beginning. We follow the One who said, "*I am* . . . the truth" (John 14:6 ESV)—not *I will show you* the truth; not *if you memorize these things*, you will have the truth; not *if you are in the right church, race, or nation*, you will know the truth. Jesus said, "*I am* . . . the truth," which means anything that does not look like God incarnate is not truth. If we let it, this truth will shatter many of our closely held deceptions that seem to protect us but in fact bring death.

The Way of Jesus

Jesus sat down on a hillside, and in the presence of multitudes, he taught his disciples about his way, the way of truth and love. If we listen carefully, we will note that not a single word in the Beatitudes relates to human notions of what a kingdom is like. Human ideas of kingdom building focus on nation, race, tribe, military strength, and wealth. Jesus teaches that greatness in his kingdom is found in the character that reflects his likeness. He begins, "Blessed are the poor in spirit" (Matt. 5:3 NIV). Happy are those who are willing to be governed by God rather than their own deceptions. Blessed are we when we are not ruled by our deceptions about power, accomplishments, and possessions or about race, hierarchy, position, and praise. We are blessed when we do the will of our Father and from that place mourn over our sins and those of others. We are humble, seeking God's thoughts about all the things we have believed that are in fact deceptions. We hunger and thirst, rejecting anything that is unlike God. We are merciful, servants to the suffering. We are pure in heart. Our hearts are undivided in obedience to the Father. We are not seeking pure theology, a pure race, or an appearance of purity. The only purity we seek is that of having a heart governed by the Lord Christ.

We easily deceive ourselves and follow false ways. We follow a caricature of Christ, one made in our image, supporting our ways and our prejudices. Odd how that Christ always seems to agree with us! Our Lord did not walk with Rome or with the Sanhedrin or with the crowds. He did not walk with his own disciples when they failed to do the will of his Father. As he said, "He who sent me is with me. He has not left me alone, for I always do the things that are pleasing to him" (John 8:29 ESV). If we follow him, then whatever we do as individuals in our families, our churches, our communities, or this world that does not look like Christ, we will both repent of and abandon. If we do not, we will look for ways to deceive ourselves into accepting what is not of God. Those deceptions can be the lies we tell ourselves about our own abuses or the abuses of others. They can also be deceptions about our pride in our positions, our teaching, or our expertise. There is a deep connection between unholy religious pride and the failure of self-control, which leaves us only too open to the worst temptations. Such things are the fruit of deception. "Whatever feeds gross personal pride promotes a swift and deadly decay of moral fiber. . . . For the person who is outwardly Christian there is no surer path to spiritual degeneracy than spiritual pride."[7]

May the "little" deaths never become comfortable and so lead us by way of self-deception to bigger deaths. May we not absorb knowledge and yet fail to obey. May we humble ourselves and seek God's face. May we call on the One who is truth to search our hearts and know our ways. May we eagerly look for the searching God who will pour out not genocide or deception or death of any kind, but rivers of living water. May we, God's people, repent.

four

The Power of Culture and the Influence of Words

Human culture is a huge and multifaceted topic, beyond the scope of this book. But it's important for our discussion of power to understand a few of the ways our culture shapes us and how it impacts our relationship to power. My work with trauma has taken me all over the world. One of the wonders of encountering other cultures is that the lens through which you see yourself and others is changed, often uncomfortably so. I have walked into cultures and seen grace and hospitality poured out like water by people who have very little of the goods of this world. I have heard music and watched dance and experienced art of many kinds, which has given me new eyes for God's beauty expressed in diverse ways. I have also had my heart broken when someone said, "Diane, incest is simply part of our culture" or when a pastor, who loves the same God I do, heatedly told me that fourteen-year-old girls who have been raped *must* marry their rapist so that the family is not shamed.

That changed lens has challenged me to look more carefully at my own culture, both secular and religious.

As humans, we are easily seduced and shaped by the culture in which we have marinated. We breathe it in constantly, and our culture becomes part of us without assessment. Its power is great and often unrecognized. That is dangerous. Because culture is simply what we know, what is familiar, we are easily blind and oblivious to the toxins we ingest that grow in and around us and that we then transmit to others. We tend not to even see how culture has shaped us. Many years ago, I heard a white pastor speak about a meeting he had with an African American pastor who told him, "You white folks don't even know you have a culture. You think your way is simply right and the rest of us have cultures." That observation exposes both the blindness and the arrogance of a dominant culture.

As children, most of us experienced going to a friend's house and observing things that were not like they were in our home. A house has no carpet, or it's dirty and chaotic, or the television is always on. Why would people live that way? We thought everyone had carpet, lived in a clean house, and watched television only at special times. Or the reverse: we were stunned by the carpet, cleanliness, and lack of television noise. Our first visit to a house of worship unlike our own or our first visit to a town or city different in size from our own is jarring. We can't imagine why others think, look, or live so differently. We also encounter some of that shock when we marry. "What do you mean," we say to our spouse, "that your family didn't do meals, or Christmas, or chores like this?" If you have traveled to or lived in another country, you have discovered that everything can be quite different: food (how it's eaten and served), speech, education, sleeping arrangements, cleanliness, marriage, faith. Our absorption of culture can be quite unconscious. Those who are unlike us are often seen as less than. We use our power to dismiss them.

As followers of Christ, we live in two cultures simultaneously. One is a secular culture. The other is the culture of Christendom. We need to be mindful of how each culture is shaping us. I fear we often absorb the culture of Christendom, with its many subcultures, denominations, and nationalities, without careful thought. We assume that what is familiar to us is the "right way" to be a Christian.

Every culture—even the culture of Christendom—is developed by people who are broken. Awareness of this foundational truth ought to result in great humility as we consider our cultures and their underlying assumptions. With the exception of Jesus Christ, every human born on this planet, every influencer and imbiber of culture anywhere, in every age since Eden, has chosen to live with self as center. George MacDonald, one of my favorite Scottish authors, puts it this way:

> For the one principle of hell is "I am my own." I am my own king and my own subject. I am the centre from which go out my thoughts; I am the object and end of my thoughts; back upon me as the alpha and omega of life, my thoughts return. My own glory is, and ought to be, my chief care; my ambition, to gather the regards of men to the one centre, myself. My pleasure is my pleasure. My kingdom is—as many as I can bring to acknowledge my greatness over them. My judgement is the faultless rule of all things. My right is—what I desire. The more I am all in all to myself, the greater I am.[1]

Any human not transformed by the redeeming work of Jesus Christ lives out of self as center. Each of our lives flows out of our own little "I am" and how that self is shaped and defined. So if I believe myself to be superior, smarter, and a gift to the world, then how I think, what I do, how I treat others, and what I pursue will flow out of that *arrogant* "I am." If I believe I am inferior, unworthy, and not capable, then how I think, what I do, how I treat others, and what I pursue will flow out of that *shattered* "I am." If I am Henry VIII and believe I am the supreme head of kingdom and church, with divine rights that cannot be questioned, then I will throw people away, chop off the heads of dissatisfactory queens, lie and steal, or do anything else I please without fearing judgment. If I am a girl who has been physically battered and sexually abused from age three to eighteen, I will be terrified, shattered, and self-protective because my "I am" is marinating in a culture of abuse. That "I am," shaped by powerful others and by our own choices, wields tremendous influence over our lives. We are in danger if we assume that self as center is not a rampant problem in Christendom.

The Danger of Good Words without Good Deeds

Our culture is expressed in many different forms. The words we use are one aspect of the shaping power of culture, influencing who we are and how we think. We live in a culture of words that are often disembodied. Words spoken but not lived out in a life, not incarnated, are untested words and can be very dangerous. We are flooded by words daily. We hear good words on social media and *assume* they are backed up by good character. Or assuming they aren't, we let loose with cruel invectives and bullying that have the potential to destroy humans created in the image of God, cruelties many of us would never speak face-to-face. We have multiplied the power of the culture of words in profound ways.

Listen to some words:

> Today Christianity stands at the head of this country. . . . I pledge that I will never tie myself to those who want to destroy Christianity. . . . We want to fill our culture again with the Christian spirit—we want to burn out all the recent immoral

development in literature, theater, the arts and in the press. . . .
In short, we want to burn out the poison of immorality which
has entered into our whole life and culture as a result of liberal
excess the past . . . few years.[2]

Take these words at face value. Do they resonate with you?
Here is what one listener said upon hearing them: "This . . .
puts in words everything I have been searching for, for years. It
is the first time someone gave form to what I want."[3] I suspect
many would say the same. There are thousands of people who,
upon hearing these words spoken, would cheer and agree and
say amen.

The words are Adolf Hitler's, and the listener was someone
in the audience who made that comment to Joseph Goebbels in
1933. Goebbels was Hitler's minister of propaganda and clearly
a very good one. Hitler's words *sound like* they are inspired by
Christian faith and morality. Listeners *assumed* a certain kind
of person stood behind them. But Hitler's words masked the
deception behind them so that those listening, without knowing
the character of the man, heard what they longed for but what
never came to fruition. What did come was the extermination of
millions, the destruction of countries, and evil that has affected
generations. The words were said to manipulate the audience
whose longings the Third Reich understood well. Hitler deliberately deceived the people and drew them in, calling forth loyalty
and service. And he got it, not just from the general population
but also from the German church. Words full of promises that
cloaked great evil were tailored for a vulnerable culture.

Using good words crafted to disguise evil is the same powerful
method used by a pedophile to groom and draw in an unsus-
pecting child. "You want to be a good girl and make Daddy
happy?" Of course she does. But in an abusive situation, there
is only hidden evil. "Hey, kid, I know things are tough at home
and your dad hits the bottle a lot. I'd like to help, so let's hang

out some, OK?" Seemingly empathic words spoken to a young boy longing for a father's attention. Words camouflaging steel jaws that will clamp down and devour a tender heart. Such words are used by a pimp with a girl on the street, a runaway from an abusive home who has nothing. "Hi, honey. You are gorgeous. Why not let me take you out to dinner?" Or they are used by traffickers luring desperate families who do not have enough to eat. "Give me your child. I'll get them a job so they can send money home. You want to help your parents out, don't you, kid?" Or they are used to cover up abuse in an institution. "He is a fabulous coach and brings money and students to the school. He put us on the map. You wouldn't want to destroy him for a little mistake, would you?" Jerry Sandusky's actions were *not* a little mistake.[4]

We are easily seduced by good words that touch our longings and desires; we frequently make the mistake of assuming those words are true because we want them to be true, not because we have seen character that demonstrates their truth. When we get glimpses, hints that raise questions, we deny the warnings because we so desperately want what we have heard to be true. So patients trust therapists, people trust pastors, students trust teachers, men and women trust each other, girls and boys trust pedophiles, and entire nations trust politicians because their words sound good. But good words can hide bad material and bad goals. Good words can whitewash evil.

Here is an exercise. Read the list of words below and make associations in your mind (or on paper) as you read. When you read a word, notice your first response. For example, if I say "love," you might think of a person's name or of words like *good* or *important* or *needed*. Here is the list:

goal oriented
ordered
efficient

productive

brilliant

unified

frugal

creative

purposeful

Would we generally think of these as good words or bad words? Would an individual, group, or institution characterized by these words accomplish a lot? Sure. Would you want someone with these characteristics in your home or company or institution? I expect so.

Now suppose I had an idea that reflected all these characteristics. I set up a plan to implement the idea, I organized it, I was creative about how to accomplish it, and I thought it was brilliant. My idea would save money and be productive. My idea would assist many people toward a good goal. I set about accomplishing my plan. I used my time, my money, and my own hands and applied my energy to achieve my goal. We teach children to do these things, yes?

But you stop by to see what I am doing and find me surrounded by human waste. I am making bricks and building structures out of human waste. They're exquisitely designed. I am saving the world money because sewer plants will no longer be necessary. My plan is frugal. I am creating housing for the poor. I am setting up a phenomenal system, providing jobs, and accomplishing a great deal in a short amount of time. My organization is brilliant. I am using my own hands, and you see focus, purpose, and creativity everywhere you look. So what's the problem? All my words still apply; all those good words are true. But you recoil. The plan is disgusting, but until you knew how I was going to flesh out my idea, it sounded good. There was nothing in my words to suggest

51

anything awful. But the material I am using to form beauty is trash, dangerous, probably disease ridden, and repulsive. Good words that describe a good process but that use the wrong substance in order to accomplish a good goal are no longer good.

When we hear scriptural words about building up the church for the glory of God, the work sounds heavenly. But when the building materials are arrogance, coercion, and aggression, the outcome is hideous. How we flesh out our good words matters.

Let's look at those characteristics again: goal oriented, ordered, efficient, productive, brilliant, unified, frugal, creative, and purposeful. Now suppose the process matches those characteristics *and* we are using the right building material. What we are using is good; it has value in and of itself. What do you think now? Suppose I am using human beings productively and have them working with wood. I am using a good substance to build strength, dignity, health, purity, and protection. I'm bringing people together to accomplish good things. I have them united, ordered, and productive for the good goal of bettering their lives. Sounds good, right?

I have just offered one description of the construction of Auschwitz, the world's largest extermination camp. "Oh, but," you say, "the Nazi goal was not good." You would be correct if by that you mean the goal of exterminating millions of human beings. But that was never the stated public goal. Hitler never stood up and told the full truth to the German people. Words were crafted to describe their goals as restoring dignity and honor to the Germans, who were humiliated after World War I, as putting bread on the shelves and giving back jobs so families would flourish, as clearing out any toxins damaging to families and society. The words named good goals. But they did not state the governing goal, which was to build the huge number of wooden barracks and the ovens at Auschwitz, where over one million human beings (labeled "pieces" in their documents) would be exterminated (which was called a "solution"). Hitler had found a "solution" for unwanted "pieces."

People use words to construct promised realities that attach to longings such as freedom, order, protection, work, or love. No abuser says, "Come with me so I can rape you." No one says, "Marry me so I can batter you." No one says, "Elect me so I can defraud you." No pastor or counselor says, "Let me counsel you so I can have sex with you." Instead, we say, "I love you." "I will protect you." "I will help you." "I will bring dignity to you." In Christendom, we can use spiritual language to cloak selfish ambition, hide abuses of many kinds, and do incalculable damage in the name of God.

Words and Integrity

Words are meant to be a true and real expression of one's character. We call this *integrity*, meaning "whole" or "entire"—no variations, no breaks, no hidden corners. James 1:17 speaks of the God of light, who does not change like shifting shadows. If I say I am a safe person, this ultimately means nothing unless you find me to be such a person consistently over time and in different places. My words do not make it so; the incarnation of safety in the flesh makes it so. We live in a culture in which leaders use the internet to share words that sound good. But when fleshed out, the words often prove to be nothing but lies.

Think about Jesus, God in the flesh. First, God has made it clear that words and flesh are to be one; there is to be integrity between words and flesh. Hence, God's words come from his essence. They reveal; they do not mask. His words and his character matched before we existed. Second, we are told that Jesus is the Word with skin on, living with us, demonstrating the character of God so that we can see and understand who he really is. God says, "I am a refuge," and Jesus sits down and holds out his arms and says, "Let the little children come to me." God says, "I am light," and Jesus brings sight to a blind man, clarity to a tormented mind, and simple, earthly explanations that help us see eternal truths. God says, "I am life," and Jesus raises back to life a little girl, the son of a widow, and a dear friend dead three days. God says, "All humans are created in my image and therefore worthy of dignity, respect, and love," and Jesus sits down with a Samaritan woman who was dehumanized on multiple levels because she was from a hated ethnicity, female (hence, inferior), and immoral. Jesus valued her, treated her with respect and kindness. *That* is how words are intended to work. God speaks words. He then demonstrates them in the flesh with full integrity so that what he says and what he lives look the same; they match. His words, his process of carrying them out through actions in relationships, and the end result are all identical. How is it that God's people use God's words to sanction things God hates?

We live surrounded by massive institutions and organizations that promise all sorts of things they never deliver, often sanctioned using God's words. They lie to cover up errors, sometimes errors they know will cause deaths. We lie to ourselves and say, "What I did was only a little thing." We tell others what they want to hear or what will get us what we want, or we are silent because we do not want to speak and cause disruption to our own lives. We lack wholeness, integrity. We think or feel one thing but often say another is true. Words are our main tool for thinking. We spend a great deal of time in our heads using words to name, to process, to assess, to discriminate. Wrong labels, deceptive words, lies, even those never spoken or heard, still do great damage. They damage us first and then that destruction proliferates out into our lives. Words are a primary tool for relating. They build, connect, and heal, or they humiliate, manipulate, and destroy. The words we say to ourselves and the words we say aloud to others need to be true and good, or we damage others and ourselves. Our words, both spoken and thought, must always be submitted to the Word made flesh and to God's written Word. Apart from an ongoing study of God's Word written and lived, we will have no true way of assessing our own words or the words of others.

Our self as center, arrogance, entitlement, and deceptive ways with words have led to polarization and dehumanization. Have we, children of the Most High God, sorted precious humans by earthly categories of politics, economics, race, gender, religion, denomination, education, employment, or citizenship? Have we created divisions as we reductively use such categories to separate, dismiss, and condemn the other? "We" are this; "they" are that.

Such categories are inadequate foundations for human identity and easily lead us to sin against others. They are not God's ultimate, foundational categories. To live governed by them is to be utterly unlike the Jesus who sat with Jews, gentiles, Samaritans, and Romans, with rich and poor, religious and secular, male and female, greeting all with truth and outstretched arms. The world's categories can so easily grip us and lead us to whitewash our reactions until we even begin to think the other should be stamped out. When others label us, we respond by catching the disease and labeling and dismissing them in return. There are many things in our culture that we as Christians must disagree with in both word and deed. But in disagreeing, we must never dismiss or dehumanize another, or we become ungodly. The bedrock category to which we can reduce another is this: a person created in the image of God and knit together by him in their mother's womb. That truth should govern our use of every other category, no matter what our particular culture has taught us.

The use of dehumanizing words is not simply a problem "out there." Observe our own churches. "They" have the wrong theology, the wrong thinking about worship, the wrong priorities.

"Our" church is, of course, biblical. Rather than dealing with our own discomfort, self-absorption, or fear of matters not going our way, we distance ourselves and label and dehumanize others. If you need more proof, observe Christians calling other Christians stupid, evil, and any number of labels on social media. Even in the face of an inevitable disagreement regarding scriptural issues, the call of that same Scripture as to how we are to treat one another is never to be tossed aside. The trashing, demeaning, humiliating, and labeling of other believers is horrifying and grieves God. A call to truth, which we must issue, is always to be done with gentleness, humility, and dignity, for we are calling one made in God's image. Opinions are not to govern character, no matter how strongly we hold them. Issues are not to govern character no matter how biblical they are. Character is to be rooted and grounded in likeness to Christ so that when we express our thoughts, we manifest his character and none other.

Yes, Jesus uses his harshest words for religious leaders. He calls them whitewashed tombs full of dead men's bones, hypocrites, and lawless. But what was his purpose in doing so? He did it out of love, turning on the light, exposing them to themselves, and calling them to himself. That harsh chapter ends with this: "O Jerusalem, Jerusalem, the one who kills the prophets and stones those who are sent to her! How often I wanted to gather your children together, as a hen gathers her chicks under her wings, but you were not willing" (Matt. 23:37 NKJV). Jesus was calling them off the edge of the cliff of their destruction. As did Ezekiel and Jeremiah before him, Jesus longed for God's people to see and return to him. Such a broken heart about another is a rare commodity in disagreements, whether in person or on Twitter.

There is no human being we will ever meet, no matter how wounded, disordered, or evil, no matter their theology, style of worship, or ways of thinking, who was not created by the God we love. Any culture—nation, denomination, city, church, or family—that leads us to treat someone otherwise is seducing us to behave in ways that break the heart of our God. The very God who crossed into our categories, bestowing dignity on all with great compassion, never dismissed those unlike himself, or we would have all been dismissed. He entered into categories that were nothing like him: male to female, Jew to gentile, holy to demon possessed. He never dehumanized us, though we had dehumanized ourselves by rejecting him who made us. He entered into our categories with truth and grace as the eternal entered the finite and the holy entered the sinful. We are to do the same in his name.

As the children of God, we are to know him so well and follow him so closely that the words swirling around us, some of them baptized by Christendom, are never allowed to silence the living and active Word in our lives. Our words are to be nothing less than the thoughts of our God. His thoughts and words became flesh so that we might see clearly who he is. He lived out before us what he spoke. We must be careful what thoughts of humankind we sanctify. And we must know that our words spoken, no matter how true, are not real unless they are incarnated.

PART 2

Power
Abused

five

Understanding Abuse of Power

We have been flooded recently with stories and headlines about power being abused in all arenas of modern life. We hear about power abused by individuals as well as by churches and organizations. These abuses all occurred in the context of relationships.

The word *relationship* derives from the Latin *referre*, meaning "brought back." It contains the idea of motion, of carrying and of bearing forth and bringing back. In this way, a relationship is like a two-way street. The word can also mean "to narrate." In other words, a relationship is a story. When we relate to others, we are cowriting a story, weaving our lives together to tell a story.

What happens when our story includes the abuse of power? The word *abuse* comes from the Latin *abuti*. It means "to misuse or use wrongly" and encompasses the ideas of exploiting, causing injury, assaulting, and perpetrating violence and offensive language. When a relationship is abusive in any form, the story being written is twisted and damaging.

Let's consider a concrete example. You live in a good neighborhood surrounded by friendly and respectful neighbors. Then the neighbors next door move away and another family moves in. You expect the new occupants to continue the weaving that has been done by your previous neighbors. But they leave junk cars and bicycles around. Sometimes they even dump their trash into your yard. You try speaking with them. They get enraged. You bring in other neighbors to no avail. Some tell you to just be quiet so the situation doesn't escalate. You go to the authorities, and they say there is nothing they can do. Your neighbors have complained that you are harassing them! Now you're living in a completely different story—mistreated, exploited, and literally "trashed." It affects your home, your marriage, your appearance, your mood, and your status. This is a small but concrete picture of what happens when abuse of any kind is brought into a relationship.

Most humans intend to use their power for good. They want to earn more money, grow the church, protect good programs, or preserve a good reputation. Adam and Eve told themselves they were pursuing a greater likeness to God. They seemed blind to the fact that they were pursuing a seemingly good goal through utterly ungodly means. We do the same thing. We tell ourselves that measures such as membership growth and financial gain in a ministry are proof of likeness to God. We then make decisions that silence unwelcome truths about fraud or abuse and tell ourselves the cover-up "preserves God's honor." We say we are using our power to seek likeness to God when in fact what we are doing looks nothing like him. It is not difficult to be seduced into such thinking. Let's consider some of the ways we might be not only abusing power but also "sanctifying" that abuse. We looked briefly at different kinds of power in chapter 1. Let's go deeper.

Physical Power

Physical power is embodied power. A man who weighs 250 pounds, stands over six feet tall, and has well-developed musculature and excellent hand-eye coordination could be a physical threat to most people. He fills the space he occupies, not just with his size but with the aura of physical strength that hangs in the air. Men and women both feel small near him. If that man is kind and godly, his strength will be welcomed and trusted, creating a sense of safety and protection. If he is abusive and full of rage, a mere touch to his wife's elbow when she says something that displeases him will elicit terror. Most people will be unaware that this simple touch communicated the warning of danger. But she knows their story. If she displeases him, his strength will be used to harm her. She will bear the impact of that harm in many ways.

In a different scenario, a person may emanate a physical presence not necessarily related to size. A presence that is scintillating, charismatic, and energetic can overwhelm. Heads turn, and the energy is felt and draws attention. Such power is less concrete but present nonetheless. A person with such power can command a room or an organization or a country. This person clearly has power to use or to abuse.

Most of us are keenly aware of the physical power of others. We have some sense of when we are vulnerable, especially when that power is obvious. We are often less aware of what our own presence communicates to others. I am especially conscious of my physical presence in my office, where I work with many clients who have abuse histories. I am quite tall, so I pay attention to where I stand and how I move so I won't overwhelm them. It is important to be aware of the impact our presence produces as well as the ways we might unthinkingly use it to control others. Whether we use our presence to overpower others or deflect attention, others will feel its impact, just as we feel the effect of their presence.

Verbal Power

Words have the power to build up or tear down a person's sense of self. A child who experiences nurturing, supportive, and kind words is far more likely to flourish than a child marinating in harsh, critical, and shaming words. That child will be crushed and may grow up silent, having no voice. Or they may become a replica of the original bully, who reached for some sense of power by verbally beating up others. Verbal bullying on social media has been linked to depression in teens, and resulting high-profile suicides have been reported.[1] Words can kill a soul. They can lead to the end of a life as well.

Sexual predators use words to groom and deceive. Words are used to cover up terrible wrongs or to control. They can seduce, condemn, humiliate, or shock. The power of words to destroy is seemingly endless. If we do not grasp the reality of verbal abuse, we will not recognize the extent of the destruction. We will excuse, minimize, or distort what is in fact crippling, deforming, shattering, and life destroying. Words can shatter the self of a child or an adult. Using words, our God-given verbal power, to control, manipulate, demean, or intimidate is abusive. It is actually not hard to crush a life by using words. Their power is staggering.

It is abuse when an adult so threatens and intimidates everyone in the home that no one dares voice a different opinion.

It is abuse when a man curses at his wife or calls her a slut, a whore, or an idiot.

It is abuse when a spouse criticizes everything about their spouse day after day—their appearance, parenting, accomplishments, and friends.

It is abuse when a parent calls a child an idiot, a good-for-nothing, or a worthless piece of trash. How long do you think a child can withstand the impact of such names before they collapse under the load?

Emotional Power

Verbal power is closely related to emotional power. I suspect that most of us have known someone whose emotions could hold a family or workplace hostage. Ever find yourself "taking someone's temperature" in order to gauge how the day will go and whether you'll need to walk on eggshells to avoid explosions or breakdowns? The governing force in that space is the emotional state of a single person. Everyone tries to act in subservience to that person's mood. This can be a powerful form of bondage.

Damaging and crushing responses to another's feelings are an example of emotional power used to abuse. A child may be afraid to go to the dentist and be humiliated for having that fear. Someone may be shamed for grieving a loss. Individuals with histories of trauma are often criticized for "still" feeling the harm of the trauma. Soldiers who suffered trauma in World War I were seen as unstable, weak, and having poor morale, their responses judged to be cowardly and a personal failure.[2] Today, even after all our study and learning about trauma, many victims are still believed to be deficient in their faith or are told to "snap out of it." Emotional abuse is, sadly, offered as a "corrective" to those with an ongoing struggle with difficult emotions.

Emotional power manifests differently when a budding dictator, someone desirous of a leadership position, or a predator wishes to gain power and control. They will work hard to understand the longings of those over whom they want control. Nations, churches, and individuals are lured into submission by assurances that what they deeply long for will become reality.

Pastors sometimes do this. "We can be the church that changes the world." People hear what they long for and follow the leader, often into disastrous circumstances. Women and men make choices about whom to marry for the same reason, hearing and responding to promises that fill them with hope. A nation devastated by war and longing for safety and prosperity will willingly follow someone who understands those powerful emotional longings and promises what is desired. Such was the case with the German church, which followed Hitler because he promised to protect Christianity and rid the nation of immorality. The church followed the man whose words gave them hope but failed to study and discern the character of the one who spoke them. Or consider a young girl who has grown up in a home filled with hatred, cruelty, and sexual abuse. She runs away at fourteen and hits the streets with no resources. A handsome, well-dressed man picks her up and takes her out to dinner. He tells her she is beautiful and buys her new clothes. His words are emotionally crafted to touch her longings. She assumes his life and his words will match, but she finds herself trapped in a desperate and abusive life worse than the one she fled.

Hooked by the dual powers of emotions and words, vulnerable people often lose their discerning capabilities and fail to see the oncoming destruction. They make assumptions when powerful promises tap into their desire, and they believe there is integrity behind the words that promise what they seek.

Powerful Combination of Knowledge, Intellect, and Skill

Having a mix of knowledge, intellect, and skill increases the likelihood that a leader will be granted unfettered, sometimes automatic authority by the people they lead. If I have more information, am smarter, or have more skills, I will have more power in certain arenas. Take, for example, my car mechanic. He has great power. When he says the thingamajig is broken and needs to be replaced, do you know what I say? "OK, how much?" Do I refuse? No, I need my car to get to work. Do I ask for a full explanation first? No, I would not understand half of it anyway. Fortunately, we have used the same mechanic for more than two decades, and he has proven to be a man of integrity, but my lack of knowledge, intellect, and skill in this area puts me at his mercy.

We often trust others in positions of authority because we assume that those with knowledge, intellect, and skill *must* be trustworthy. But that is not always the case. The power that comes with knowledge, intellect, and skill can be abused.

Larry Nassar, a physician for young gymnasts, was esteemed for his "specialized" knowledge and skill that allowed him to assist athletes in their training. Young girls were brought to him by the dozens for him to heal their injuries and help them perform. He knew what was wrong and how to fix it. He was also the most prolific known pedophile in sports history. His expertise was renowned and his good character was assumed, even as women and young girls reported abuse to almost every possible authority for about twenty years.[3]

The power of knowledge applies to the theological or spiritual realm, where a degree in theology can give someone "theological power" over others. We assume that this expert knows more, so we give them the right to tell the rest of us what is true about God and ourselves and to speak authoritatively about our marriages, our children, our work, or how we handle our money. But Scripture can be twisted and used out of context to corrupt or to control people who assume that the pastor is a trustworthy person. The power of a pastor is intensified by the fact that many see a minister as speaking *for* God; indeed, a pastor may tell people that they are doing exactly that. So when a male pastor says to a woman, "God says you should go home to the man who is battering you and love him better," she says, "OK." The woman assumes the pastor speaks truth because of his theological knowledge and because he is the mouthpiece of God. Some women have been killed while following such horrific advice.

The seductive trio of knowledge, intellect, and skill carry great weight and often lead to trust, earned or not. Larry Nassar was a doctor, Jerry Sandusky was a coach, and Bill Hybels was a pastor. They were able to exclude, fire, publicly shame, and ostracize any vulnerable patient, player, or parishioner. They were able to cover up, to overreach, to rename actions, and to sway others.

If you want some sense of the power associated with knowledge, intellect, and skill, listen carefully to others when they speak: "My doctor said," "My boss said," "My pastor said." Hear the assumption of that person's authority embedded in what people say. Knowledge, intellect, and skill render credibility but without any certainty of the character of the one who possesses them.

Economic Power

Money, property, and other resources are closely associated with power. Economic power promises and often delivers a certain measure of security and comfort. It can also be used to control, manipulate, and intimidate another person. Money and resources are used as weapons.

Denise had been married twenty-five years and had three children. Her husband was wealthy. He was also abusive verbally, emotionally, physically, and financially. He had complete control over her access to economic resources. All of "their" many properties, including their home, were in his name, as was every checking and savings account. She had a very limited credit card with both of their names on it and was forbidden to go over a set amount. If anyone ran a credit check, there would essentially be no record for her. She simply did not exist. Her vulnerability was staggering. A lack of access to money prevented her from leaving, even as she feared for her life.

Economic abuse occurs in many marriages. The one in control can use their economic power to enforce conformity to demands, no matter how extreme. Economic abuse can also happen to the elderly or to those who have trust funds managed for them. Resources can be stolen or moved, and wills can be changed. I've worked with clients whose parents, grandparents, or spouses managed assets in humiliating and controlling ways, leaving my clients feeling small, owned, and insignificant. Economic abuse can also occur when one partner leeches off another. Oftentimes they claim to be looking for a job, but in actuality they are not. This dance can go on for decades. It can happen when someone receives an inheritance or was wealthy prior to the marriage and is blind to the fact that they are simply being used for their financial resources. Like physical abuse, many forms of economic abuse are illegal.

How we use our economic power exposes who we are. In the workplace, money can be used to get people to work horrendous hours. It can be a power factor in friendships in which one friend always pays, making inequality foundational to the relationship and creating a financial imbalance that the person with the bigger purse can use to control and humiliate.

Power and Sex

I have written two books on sexual abuse and spoken on the topic more times than I can count, so a summary is challenging.[4] Sexuality is one of the most vulnerable aspects of being human, and it is present from birth to death. Sexuality is integrally tied to both identity and intimacy, and the potential for damage is extremely high.

Sexual abuse is generally defined as any sexual activity—verbal, visual, or physical—that is engaged in without consent. A child victim is considered unable to consent due to developmental immaturity and an inability to understand sexual behavior. When we are talking about adults, it is important to understand what makes something consensual. First, in order to consent, one must have the capacity to choose. If you are anesthetized in a hospital bed, you obviously do not have that capacity. The intoxicated young woman in a previous chapter did not have the capacity to choose. If your whole self has been anesthetized by years of sexual abuse, battering, verbal tirades, or drugs or alcohol, you do not have that capacity—it has been trampled, killed. Second, consent means it is safe to say no. If you are five and he is forty, if he is the boss and can fire you, if someone has the power to ostracize you from your community, consent is not possible because it is not safe to say no.

Verbal sexual abuse includes things such as sexual threats, sexual comments about one's body, lewd remarks, harassment, and suggestive comments. Verbal sexual abuse can also be more covert. When it is subtle, the victim may be confused and feel uncertain about the inappropriateness of a comment. Sexual or provocative language has no place in a parent/child, teacher/student, pastor/parishioner, coach/athlete, employer/employee relationship.

Visual sexual abuse includes the viewing or the making of pornographic material, exhibitionism (displaying oneself sexually), and voyeurism (secretly watching others undress or engage in sexual activity for one's own sexual gratification).

Physical sexual abuse includes intercourse, oral and anal sex, digital penetration, masturbation in front of someone or of another person, and the fondling of breasts and genitals, again without consent.

Sexual abuse is frighteningly common. One in four girls and one in six boys are sexually abused by the age of eighteen.[5]

Such abuse is frequently unreported, so the statistical reality is not fully known. Sexual abuse happens in homes, churches, schools, service organizations, hospitals, camps, and retirement homes; in cars and on public transportation; and in the offices of doctors, professors, and coaches.

The revelation of sexual abuse is never welcome, certainly not by victims and often not by those who are asked to help, for it's a world we do not want to enter. We would rather cross to the other side of the road, convincing ourselves we are doing so for a righteous and just reason. As Jesus taught us, such responses are telling. The abuse exposes the heart of the abuser, not the heart of the victim. The refusal to help exposes those asked, not the victim. The asking exposes the courage of the victim.

A Story of Abuse

Kenny Stubblefield is a filmmaker, a survivor of clergy sexual abuse, and an advocate for fellow victims.[6] With his permission, I will share some of his story here.

Kenny grew up attending church. He was taught at home and at church about being loved by and loving Jesus. His parents were loving and actively supportive. Kenny was sixteen years old when he formed a bond with an associate youth pastor. The pastor was college-age and acted in ways that divided friends against each other. He determined who was accepted and popular by inviting boys to his home. Kenny longed to be chosen. He wanted to be accepted. One day it finally happened. The pastor invited him for a sleepover. He and Kenny hung out in the back den near the pastor's bedroom. The pastor began flipping channels on the television, "accidentally" stopping on pornographic shows. He acted shocked but still tarried a bit before changing the channel. Unknown to Kenny, grooming had begun.

Kenny asked to sleep on the couch. The answer was no. How about on the floor in the living room? Again, the answer was no. The pastor said Kenny needed to share his waterbed. Kenny woke up during the night feeling the youth pastor's hands on his genitals. Assuming it was accidental, he moved them. It was not an accident. The touching continued throughout the night. Kenny did what most of us would do in such a situation; he panicked and froze. He did not go back to sleep and decided it must somehow be his fault, a common response. He decided silence would be safest, certain that no one would take his word over the word of a pastor (he guessed right). A year later, while speaking with his best friend, he discovered that his friend had also been abused. After learning about yet another victim, Kenny went to the head youth pastor to tell him that he and two of his friends had been abused by the associate. As Kenny says, "My nightmare had just begun."[7]

The youth pastor was angry with the victims because by exposing the abuse, "they" were damaging "his" ministry. The associate was fired, but no legal action was taken, no care was offered to the victims, and no public warning was given regarding the predator. The senior pastor ended the episode with a sentence that would control the next two decades of Kenny's life: "If you want to be faithful, you will be quiet."[8]

Years later, all three victims wrote to the senior pastor about the abuse they had endured. There was no response. Instead, the pastor contacted lawyers. The church leadership proceeded to lie from the pulpit, denying the abuse and burying the truth.

In spite of it all, Kenny has lived and is still living redemptively. He dragged the abuse and its cover-up into the light and called it by its right name. He called for truth and righteousness and justice. He has become a voice and an advocate for those silenced by abuse. He is also a voice of truth regarding those who would protect the abusers. He does not cross to the other side of the road but instead keeps returning for yet more of the vulnerable and wounded. I am grieved by what happened to Kenny and what happened to those he's now helping. I am also grateful for his life, his courage, and his voice.

Final Thoughts

It is important to note that many people suffer from multiple kinds of abuse, often all at once. You can experience sexual abuse, verbal and emotional abuse, and abuse by someone trusted by virtue of their knowledge. The damage is of course exponential. It is also greatly increased when a cry for help results in more abuse. The use of verbal and emotional mistreatment to silence a victim, coupled with power used to prevent exposure of an abuser, can have catastrophic outcomes in a vulnerable life. The combined abuses constitute a life-destroying tsunami. The fact that those in the body of Christ commit these abuses, and then use the name of God to cross over to the other side of the road, is frankly horrific.

I challenge you to consider the various arenas of power we have discussed. Which types of power were abused in Kenny's story? They are all there, even economic power, because I am quite certain that part of the church's motivation was to protect its assets, its monetary power. His story also includes two kinds of power we have not yet named: spiritual and systemic. These will be discussed in future chapters. Consider the life-forming burden of this tsunami of abuses placed on the back of an adolescent. It was put there with the "help" of those who name the name of Christ. In direct disobedience to God's call to bend down and bear Kenny's burden *with him*, they increased it instead. Kenny's life is a clarion call to the church, a call to repentance and humility. His life is being used by God to expose us to ourselves. I pray we will listen.

six

Power in Human Systems

Many people think the abuse of power happens only between individuals. But *systems* can also be abusive. Systemic abuse occurs when a system, such as a family, a government entity, a school, a church or religious organization, a political group, or a social service organization, enables the abuse of the people it purports to protect. Even when acts of abuse are perpetrated solely by an organization's leader, his or her behaviors tend to be perpetuated by a systemic organizational response with the goal of preserving the system in reaction to a perceived threat.

What is a system? A system is a combination of parts that work together, forming a complex unitary whole. In the mechanical world, a vacuum cleaner is a system. All the parts work together for the purpose of cleaning rugs. In an investment system, all the parts work together to grow wealth. A system can also be defined by a set of doctrines or principles used to explain the working arrangement of the whole, as when many parts of the global church came together under the Lausanne Covenant. Systems, even mechanical ones, are generally designed to serve groups of people.

The word *system* comes from two Greek words meaning "together" and "stand." Human systems "stand together" for an ostensibly good purpose. Abuse, as we know, means "to misuse or use wrongly." So systemic abuse applies when a system that is designed to serve people is instead destroying them, reducing, harming, wasting, and dehumanizing those created in the image of God. Dignity, vibrancy, impact, creativity, building, and producing are silenced and crushed. This distortion results in the parts of the system standing together to serve the system rather than the people.

When systemic abuse occurs in an organization theoretically unified around a good purpose, the overt or stated purpose is not in fact the governing one. For abusive conduct to be perpetrated by agents of a system, that conduct must be facilitated by fundamental, though often hidden, properties of the system itself. In other words, a susceptibility to abuse is built in at some underlying level of the system's architecture. Any godly response to abuse requires restorative actions that work toward the recovery of the image of God that has been distorted.

Systemic Abuse of Power in Action

Let's look more closely at systemic abuse to gain a greater understanding of what it is and how different parts of a system contribute to or support abusive actions. Consider Burma, now known as Myanmar, which was governed for years by a brutal, self-serving, tyrannical regime. I have worked with abused people as well as with abusive families, communities, and churches for decades. But my experience in Burma was the first time I entered into and witnessed an entire nation being abused. The ruling generals used oppression, brutality, force, intimidation, unpredictability, and isolation to control the people. It worked.

A Burmese gentleman described to me examples of the leaders' strategy. One day the people of Myanmar woke up and were instructed, on the whim of the top general, to drive on the opposite side of the road. This edict had to be changed back quickly due to the overwhelming number of accidents. He also told me that all Burmese get a retirement pay equivalent to ten cents per month—and that it costs twenty cents to ride the bus to the only bank where they can collect the retirement pay. The country has purposeless forced labor. I watched men and women carry heavy boulders from one side of the road to the other and then be forced to carry them back. These and many other abuses exemplified the oppression, mind control, destruction of purpose, silencing of voice, destruction of relationship, and crushing of personal power that constitute systemic abuse. The system is so powerful and controlling that the country's governance looks like insanity to an outsider. Obedience means accepting the delusion that such things are reasonable. The wills of the people have been repeatedly broken, their choices removed, their minds numbed, and their trust destroyed. The military junta has relentlessly destroyed those created in the image of God until only shells remain. Burma is an extreme example, as is Nazi Germany, but both are pictures of systemic abuse that help us understand it in less obvious situations.

Many men have come forward to talk about their victimization as minors while in a Boy Scouts of America (BSA) troop. A recent report states that more than twelve thousand Boy Scout members were victims of sexual abuse at the hands of almost eight thousand alleged perpetrators.[1] The stated purpose of this organization is to assist young men in making ethical and moral choices. It is one of the largest youth organizations in the United States and has done much good. But even an organization with lofty goals can fall prey to systemic abuse. So-called perversion files were kept by the Boy Scouts since the 1920s.[2] Many of these files expose collaboration between the

BSA leadership and other systems (police chiefs, prosecutors, pastors) to cover up abuses for the sake of the organization— multiple systems colluding in actions completely opposed to the organization's stated purposes. The corruption flowed down from the top. A permissive stance toward abuse at BSA head-quarters also spread to the systems under its leadership. The choices of those with power filtered into the smaller systems functioning under them. A system established to teach ethical and moral principles joined with the systems of justice and faith, and together they made immoral, unethical, and unjust choices. Clearly, the hidden purpose of protecting the system ultimately governed the actions of the system rather than its stated purpose. The BSA was destroying itself, believing it was preserving an ethical, moral system by making unethical and immoral choices.

As I write, more news has come to light regarding the BSA. Peter Janci, an abuse lawyer and advocate, says, "Based on scientific literature regarding significant underreporting of abuse by victims and high levels of recidivism by perpetrators, within a system that minimized and concealed abuse, I estimate the number of #boyscoutabuse victims is well over 100,000."[3]

We are also painfully aware of reports in recent years about systemic abuse in faith communities. Catholics, Jews, Protestants, Muslims, and Mormons all have a stated purpose to glorify God and serve him faithfully. Yet so many religious systems have worked to cover up abuse, deny abuse, and protect the offenders. Many have done so "to protect God's work," which actually translates into preserving an institution rather than the humans meant to flourish in it.

Churches, schools, orphanages, and faith-based institutions have protected organizations, power, position, wealth, race, ethnicity, and many other things. The larger system, denomination, or association affects or infects smaller systems of individual churches and families; so, if church leaders are actively abusive or if they sanction or ignore domestic abuse or sexual abuse, the implied permission to abuse power reaches into family systems. It is clear that we have preferred our organizational trappings to the holiness of God. We have guarded our material treasures rather than the treasure of human beings. Talk about self-injury and disastrous consequences. Destroy the children and there will be no future.

Complicity with a System

The more desperate people are, the more eager they will be for a champion to ride in on a white horse and make everything better. People in these circumstances are vulnerable to control and manipulation. They rightly long for a messiah but may blindly follow an imposter, until the reality behind the leader's stated purpose is exposed and they realize they were duped.

The leader is a key component of any system, from a Stalin or a Hitler to a powerful charismatic preacher or a dominating father. The leader usually has a group of close followers whose access to the leader gives them power in the system. These are the insiders, the ones in the know, a coterie of elders or board members, wealthy donors or church members of a favored gender, race, or ethnicity who exert excessive influence in the system. They work hard to protect their positions and the power that goes with them. The leaders and these close groups are overtly and often passionately committed to the organization's stated mission. But it is very easy to get caught up in the trappings of power and personal gain, settling for mere preservation of the system that provides those benefits.

Followers with less power but with an unquestioning belief in and active protection of leadership make up another component of the system. These people have accepted the idea that "we" in this institution are special and that the system needs to be protected at all costs. In faith settings, they are the ones who use Scripture to support power and keep the leaders in place. These church members alienate others who question leadership or, worse yet, who bring allegations of wrong actions or abuse. In Rwanda, they were the neighbors who believed the leaders' genocide propaganda was a way to "preserve" the nation. In places like Afghanistan, they are the men who attack the "lesser gender," seen as a threat to the system simply because they seek an education.[4] These followers serve the cause and in doing so destroy themselves and relinquish their own voices, trustworthiness, and power. By their compliance and obedience, they align themselves with the powerful, acting according to their dictates and seemingly functioning to protect the system but actually destroying it from within.

Others in the system are not compliant by words or action but by blindness. Sadly, we've all been party to this kind of passivity—the turning of the head, a denial of reality. *Surely it cannot be true*, we think, and we choose comfort rather than causing a disturbance. Families in which the spouse protects the abuser by "not seeing" are compliant by blindness. In churches across this nation, children have said, "Someone touched me," not even understanding what was done to them, and in response, law-abiding citizens of heaven have said, "This doesn't happen in our church. It cannot be true because the accused person is so nice, and teaches Sunday school, and would never do anything like that." Instead of facing the truth, they discredit and ignore. Why? Because acknowledging the truth will completely disrupt the system.

We don't believe that the powerful leaders we admire could possibly abuse their power. We don't want to see because if we see, we must either act or carry the guilt of not having done so. We don't want to see because it threatens our belief in the virtue of our leaders and the worth of the system. The leadership is perceived as good, based on what is said, preached, taught, or promised, and we tell ourselves that's the whole truth.

We also dread the harm of exposure. What will happen if this truth is known? It will ruin the reputation of the group. Or worse, it will damage the name of Christ. "This is his work; we cannot ruin it." We believe institutions such as church and family are God ordained and therefore must be protected at all costs. So we cover and deny. We react with disbelief, minimizing, and lying to self and others. Rather than calling it clergy sexual abuse, we call it a misunderstanding. We would rather believe a reassuring lie than an utterly inconvenient and disturbing truth. We protect the system by shielding the accused. We say we do not want to falsely accuse. But we are not as adamant about the failure to protect victims. Vulnerable humans need protection in every human system. There is no system so godly that this is not true. Vulnerable ones need a voice, yet they're easily discounted by virtue of their vulnerability. We give credibility to those who are not afraid, have confidence, and seem important to sustaining the system. We give more credibility to power.

Let's go back to the Boy Scouts of America. Someone had to report the abuse for those perversion files to exist. Victims had to speak. Then BSA leadership faced a choice: to respond to it or bury it. They chose protection from exposure rather than protection of children. These decisions involved many people and lasted for decades, hidden away until victims began to speak out in public for themselves. This has been true in countless churches, missions, orphanages, and Christian schools.

In the Christian world, we deny what we hear because we want to protect the name of Jesus. If word gets out that someone is committing fraud, abusing children, beating his wife, or treating group members in nasty, bullying, and ostracizing ways, then the reputation of Jesus will be marred, and we must prevent that. How can it ever be wrong to protect the name of Jesus? See how we can use godly words to cover ungodly deeds?

In Christian circles, we *say* we're doing the work of the Lord; we're protecting *his* work. We'd do well to recall that the prophet Jeremiah called out the Israelites for repeating "the temple of the LORD" as they worshiped idols. "Do not trust in deceptive words and say, 'This is the temple of the LORD, the temple of the LORD'" (Jer. 7:4 NIV). God's response was a call to righteousness. He called them to make their ways healthy and to stop tolerating sin in their midst. The prophet spoke to the sick, sinful system all that God had commanded him to speak, and the system's response was to demand the death of the truth teller, saying *he* must die. They wanted to render *him* mute. That is exactly what systems try to do to dissidents, truth tellers, or their victims. They work to silence them.

No system that carries oppression, silencing, dehumanizing, violence, abuse, and corruption within is healthy, no matter how godly the goals of that system may be. Tolerance of such things, out of fear, disbelief, or self-deception, will not protect the system from the disease that will kill it if left untreated.

We often confuse the system of Christianity (Christendom) with Christ. But no so-called Christian system is truly God's work unless it is full of truth and love. To tolerate sin, pretense, disease, crookedness, or deviation from the truth is to do something other than the work of God, no matter the words used to describe it. As humans, we tend to submit to the command of other humans, to tradition, or to culture, refusing to listen to and obey the living and ever-present God. Chanting "This is the temple of the LORD" or "This is God's work" does not make it so. Proclaiming with the Boy Scouts "We teach morals and ethics" while covering immorality is an indicator that the system is no longer moral. Nor are those who hide its immorality.

Some of us have faced the power of systems that proclaim God's name yet look nothing like him. That power can be formidable. It's hard to fight an organic whole, particularly when a system is full of people we love or those important to us and our future. We have seen the power of such systems in Nazi Germany and the Boy Scouts. It was there in the system of slavery in the US and in the slavery of sex trafficking today. The system sweeps others along into participating in its corrupt ways. How much easier it is to keep quiet and go along, especially when the system has been about doing good work in the name of God. We forget that anything done in the name of God that does not bear his character through and through is not of him at all. In our forgetting, we are more loyal to the words of humans than to the commandments of God.

It is vital for us to keep in mind that the purpose of *any* system is for people to stand together to protect, serve, or nurture human beings, who are created in the image of God. This applies to all systems, including governments, corporations, communities, town councils, tribes, and families. The system is for the people; the people do not serve the system. They are not its subjects. They are, whether they know it or not, servants of the Most High God and him alone. All systems are to be subject to him. When they are not, they no longer serve the people, nor are they God approved.

It is easy to become confused about this in a God-ordained system. Take the example of marriage, a God-ordained institution. When marital violence is exposed, church leaders may send the victim of that violence home to "suffer for Jesus's sake" in what they see as an effort to protect the sanctity of marriage. But violence has already shattered sanctity. What they're attempting to protect is not actually a marriage except in name. It is a war zone that is destroying all occupants.

When the Israelites tried to protect the temple despite its corruption, God responded with the equivalent of blasting them out of Israel. He didn't preserve the structure because his temple is ultimately in the hearts of people, not in a system. Israel as a nation was bringing sacrifices into the temple even while it was rotting at its core and destroying the very people it was meant to protect. God does not preserve form without regard for content. God wants purity in the kingdom of the heart, not the appearance of it in a system. Our systems, our countries, our faith groups, our tribes, and our organizations are *not* the kingdom of God. He resides in the hearts of his people, who are called to love and obey him even when our structures, institutions, and systems fall down around us.

Responding to Abusive Systems

So how should we respond to systemic abuse? It begins with facing the truth. Consider what a healthy response to a physical symptom looks like. A person discovers a lump on their body; they can choose to ignore the lump or to take action to protect their physical system. When a response is driven by fear of what the lump might indicate and how disruptive or painful treatment might be, the person may hide the facts from themselves, denying the presence of the lump even though it could cost them their health or even their life. But if they face the truth and do what is necessary to address the symptoms, they can bring healing to their body.

In considering instances of power abused in systems, we are dealing with diseases of abuse, violence, and oppression, of immorality, fraud, and corruption. We can expend energy keeping up appearances and preserving the system while ignoring the disease. We may believe that if we drop the pretense, acknowledge the disease, and work to stop it, we will in fact destroy the system. But disguising the symptoms of the sickly system is no step toward recovery.

Jesus lived as part of a dominated group of people under a pervasive system of government. Rome ruled the world by sheer force and power. That larger system was made up of many sub-groups: Jews and gentiles, lepers and clean, male and female, religious leaders and ordinary folk. The religious people had their own subgroups of scribes, Pharisees, and Sadducees. All the religious systems were corrupt. They dehumanized people, isolated and excluded people, and crushed people with heavy burdens. An "us versus them" distinction was firmly enforced. The outgroups ("them") included Samaritans, lepers, beggars, and women. By Roman standards, all Jews were "them." Children were property, like slaves. Infanticide, abandonment, and abuse were common.

God is not silent regarding systemic abuse. He sent Jesus, who lived in the midst of these corrupt systems, and I believe that in Jesus God speaks in a dissenting voice about systemic abuse. A dissident is a person who opposes official policy. A dissident is one who disagrees. The term became popular when the Soviet Union was in power. We defined a system as people standing together. Jesus *sat apart* from those who stood together in his day. It is quite a picture, isn't it? In the same manner and spirit of Jesus, all Christians should be dissidents in the corrupt systems of this world, including in our own beloved institutions.

There are many examples of the dissidence of Jesus. In his day, Jews harbored systemic racial prejudice toward Samaritans. And a Jewish man prayed daily, thanking God for not having made him a woman. Jesus, sitting at a well in the land of "them," was thirsty. We are told there came a woman of Samaria. She was a double no-no. This woman was a "them among thems," having been through five husbands and currently cohabiting with a sixth man. She was from the hated group, was the despised gender, and was immoral. But the Son of Man saw her humanity just as he saw humanity under leprous scales, just as he saw humanity in little children (John 4:7–26).

Nearly all Jesus's miracles were interventions on behalf of life. He intervened for those who were oppressed, abused, diseased, endangered, and traumatized. He did not dissent in the

85

American way or in any other way with which we are familiar. He carried no placard emblazoned with hateful speech. He gave to Caesar what was his, tyrant though he was. The coin had Caesar's picture on it; Caesar could have the coin. But Jesus ever and always gave to God what was God's, which was himself and broken humanity with him. He stood against anything and everything that deformed, crushed, and destroyed humanity, including religious leaders. His woes to the leaders echo the woes of God in Ezekiel 34: "Woe, shepherds of Israel who . . . with force and severity . . . have dominated [the sheep]. . . . I am against the shepherds, and I will demand My sheep from them" (vv. 2, 4, 10 NASB). In Matthew 23, he speaks damning words to the leaders of a centuries-old religious institution originally ordained by God himself, saying, "Woe to you, scribes and Pharisees, . . . you devour widows' houses . . . [but neglect] justice and mercy and faithfulness" (vv. 13–14, 23 ESV).

In his meeting with the Samaritan woman, Jesus crossed the lines between Jew and Samaritan, male and female, pure and impure. He ignored nationalism, racial prejudice, gender bias, and rules for clean and unclean. We see his dissidence in his relentless seeking of people, no matter where they were. He pursued them with love and truth. He pursued them one by one.

Systemic abuse is a formidable and insidious force. Nations destroy their own people and the people of other nations. Corporations pursue greed, gorging on the wealth found in God's earth. Communities self-destruct, and neighbor kills neighbor. Churches and religious systems ostracize and crush children who have been abused, those who have been raped, and those who live with other forms of violence. They do so to preserve a system they call God's. Families eat each other alive with rape and incest and violence. We are God's dissidents every time we respond in offices, in communities, in churches, in schools, and in any areas of abuse. We do this as a part of systems, many of them with good and godly aims. We must not go to sleep. We must watch. We must not assume that our family, church, community, country, or organization is always right just because the people in it use the right words. We must never agree to "protect" the name of God by covering ungodliness. In Ephesians 5:11, Paul warns us not to participate in the deeds of darkness but instead to expose them. Understand that you cannot singlehandedly change an entire system; you are not called to do so. Yet we are to speak truth about our systems. This is difficult to do and sometimes quite risky. Just ask Martin Luther King Jr. Ask Martin Luther himself. Ask those in the #MeToo movement. When systems change, it is often little by little and usually at great cost.

When you feel overwhelmed, remember this: people are sacred, created in the image of God. Systems are not. They are only worth the people in them and the people they serve. And people are to be treated, whether one or many, the way Jesus Christ treated people. He made them more vibrant and human; he *never* dehumanized. He joined with; he became like us. He never divided humans into us and them. He never treated people as pathogens. He worked righteousness into hearts and lives.

What does all this mean for us as we live within systems and desire to please God? It means we must be poured out like salt, an aseptic, free from infection and pathogens. As Christians, we are to be a healthy immune system in the world. As we walk with Christ in love and obedience, no matter the cost to our habits and preferences or our favored systems, we are to live as he did, uncorrupted in this corrupted world. We are to be light in the darkness, exposing those things that are not like God no matter where we find them, even in those organizations we greatly love. We are called to sit apart when those who stand together are disobedient to him.

We must keep two things in mind when facing the overwhelming force and power of this world's systems. First, we must be so soaked in and shaped by the Word of our God that we are able to see the truth and call it by its right name. Marinated in our own cultures and traditions, both secular and religious, shaped by generations of our own families, we are bent and twisted by those systems. It is easy for us to see those outside, the "them" who are parts of other systems, as wrong, evil, or simply less than. We need the truth of the written Word of God and of the Word of God made flesh to help us see how to live out what God says, or we will lose our way, interpreting the written Word through the lens of culture and tradition and easily bending what is written to our own ends. Jesus came both to do and to teach. We must listen carefully and watch him closely. We must not divorce the two.

Second, we must recognize that the change of massive systems always comes one person at a time. It is God's way. Change looks impossible, frankly hopeless. But our God calls his people, multiplies them, and brings transformation. Abraham, Moses, Ruth, David, Esther, Elijah, Peter, John, Mary Magdalene, Paul, Priscilla, you, me. Jesus himself came as one man. He grants his Spirit to us one by one and calls us to follow in his footsteps, bearing his fragrance and speaking truth and grace to this world one by one. The multiplying of that work is his work, not ours.

The kingdoms of this earth are many and have been used to increase power, to kill, and to make self-serving "moral" judgments. Political systems and economic systems have all promised freedom and equality and growth and yet have crushed humans created in the image of God. Our institutions, organizations, educational systems, and, yes, Christendom have all abused power, trashed vulnerable members, and turned blind eyes, all seemingly for the greater good. And our own beloved systems—our families, churches, esteemed halls of learning, and special clubs—have all protected the system at the expense of at least a lamb or two.

But one by one, light breaks through and change comes.

The Atlantic slave trade, segregation in US schools, and the Nazi regime were all powerful systems that were changed by one person—William Wilberforce, Martin Luther King Jr., Dietrich Bonhoeffer—influencing others.

Here is another one-by-one story. Some of my father's family came from Switzerland and eventually landed in West Virginia, where they owned and operated salt and coal mines. The Ruffner family established Charleston, West Virginia, and, to my great grief, had enslaved people working in the mines.

Booker T. Washington was the son of enslaved people.[5] After emancipation, this little boy worked in the salt mines, carrying one-hundred-pound sacks filled with grains of salt. His first encounter with school was standing outside and looking wistfully in the windows at other children learning. At age ten he was assigned as a houseboy to Viola Ruffner, wife of the owner of the mines. She observed his intelligence and eagerness to learn, helped him learn to read, and gave him time off each day to attend school.

Washington went on to establish the Tuskegee Institute as a leading college in the United States. He spoke out on race relations during the Jim Crow era and was the first African American invited to the White House. My ancestor could not stop slavery. She could not change race relations in this country. She could not educate all the children of enslaved people, children who should have been educated. But she helped one son of slavery, and her action was multiplied beyond anyone's expectations. One by one, thousands of lives and many generations were changed because a little boy learned to read. In the same way, we are to be a presence in the systems of the world for the glory of God.

So remember this: it is vital that you see truly and clearly and call things by their right names. Do not be anesthetized by so-called good systems, controlled by bad ones, or complicit by a deliberately chosen blindness. Do not sit down hopeless, thinking the problem is too big and change will never come. Put your roots down deep into the Word of God written and made flesh. Bow before the One who rules the kingdoms of heaven and earth so that he might make you into his likeness. And then, like him, go out and speak and touch and love and help one by one, full of his grace and truth. He will multiply what you do.

Ignore the lines the world draws and love the least of these— the little ones, the vulnerable, the abused, the traumatized, the trafficked, and the discarded. *That* is how you speak truth to power. That is how you disciple and bless the nations, one by one among the least of these. It is small work, often hidden and slow. But it is God's work until the day comes when the only system left standing is made up of those who love and follow Christ. It is God's work until the seventh angel sounds the trumpet and loud voices in heaven say, "The kingdoms, the systems of this world have become the kingdom of our Lord and Christ, and he will reign forever and ever" (Rev. 11:15).

seven

Power between Men and Women

I grew up in the 1950s and '60s, lively years in which traditional and proper met hippies and drugs. Following college graduation in 1970, I studied at the Swiss L'Abri Fellowship under evangelical theologian and philosopher Francis Schaeffer. I returned to the States and earned a PhD in psychology, the only female in my class of seven. By the time that decade ended, I had two degrees, a husband, and one of our two sons.

Through all of this, I was also a part of Christendom. It has been an interesting, sometimes hurtful, and often blessed ride. I grew up with loving Christian parents who actively nurtured my brain and told me I could be anything I set my mind to. Because my father was in the military, we moved often and attended a wide variety of churches. As a result, I experienced many cultures, both secular and Christian, and that experience was an inestimable gift that nurtured my understanding and belief that worship is about a person named Jesus Christ. He is the One on the throne, and our obedience is to him alone, not a leader, a denomination, or a church.

While I was in graduate school, many Christian men informed me that I was wrong to get graduate degrees. My gifts, they told me, were given to me by God to be used for a husband and children and then *perhaps* in the church. They recommended I get married (I was not in a relationship at the time) and leave graduate school. Thankfully, my father reminded me of my abilities and my freedom to choose. I worked for a Christian psychologist for several years who treated me well and asked me to do some public speaking with him. Neither of us was prepared for the pushback. Responses ranged from "She cannot come" to "She can come but cannot speak to men," "She can come but has to wear a hat," "She can come but must speak from the floor, not the stage." You get the picture. He advocated for me; I often stooped to accommodate others, and away we went.

When I began counseling in the early 1970s, I encountered women who spoke in vague, hesitant terms about abuse. Nobody used the word *abuse*. Domestic abuse "did not happen" because men were believed to have more credibility. Rape was considered the fault of the female. Women asked to see me because I was female, not because I knew anything. I was twenty-three. I listened, asked questions, and told them honestly that I knew nothing and would have to be their student first. I was told by male supervisors not to believe their hysterical stories and lies about "good" men.

I chose to listen to the women rather than to my supervisors.

I was also counseling returning Vietnam veterans. I noticed two things. First, the vets returning from war and the wives coming to me in secret had the same symptoms. I concluded that there was more than one kind of war zone. I grew up knowing about combat but not about war in the home. Second, abused women got smaller, as if the self was literally shrinking, while the vets seemed to get bigger. They were often hard drinkers, angry, and violent. The violence occurred mostly at home, but some could not contain themselves enough to hold a job. What I came to understand was twofold. Males are taught to be strong, competent, and in charge; their authority is to be obeyed. Females are taught to yield, support, and nurture. The tasks are not interchangeable. Hence, violence is the male's right, and the burden of managing it is the female's.

I realized that the victims of abuse were not the only ones losing the person God created them to be. The abusers were also diminished as they yielded to violence. War zones make everyone feel little. Power abused is power used for control and coercion of the victim. What is often not understood is that power abused is also power out of control, which is, by definition, powerlessness. Those who are violent and abusive are powerless to control themselves. Those who are victims are powerless to change the violent one.

Abuse of power is a cancer in the body of Christ. How Christendom uses terminology regarding gender is sometimes an aspect of the disease. We need to let the light of a holy God expose us and our systems. A man named Jesus had nothing to do with these ways. He used his power without abuse, coercion, or complicity. A male named Jesus interacted with all kinds of women and protected, blessed, healed, encouraged, and lifted them up. He never told them to submit to evil or wrongdoing. He didn't silence them. Much of masculinity in Christendom looks nothing like Jesus. It has been contaminated by secular culture and sanctioned using theological terms. Any theology that does not produce the fruit of Jesus is false. We are doing great damage to countless vulnerable people and to God's church because people destroyed by abuse perpetrated by the powerful cannot use the fullness of their God-given gifts to bless his body. Those perpetrating the abuse are not gifting the church as God intended either. We simply keep repeating theological words almost like a mantra: *leader*, *head*, *submission*, *authority*, *God ordained*. We need to drag into the light those things we cover with familiar and good words and test them to see whether our labels and our applications are of God. Many are not.

We use our theological mantras when faced with a battered woman who has no access to money and gets tied to the bed whenever the man, who considers himself her "head," wants to have sex. We use these words when a thirteen-year-old comes forward and says that his youth pastor taught him about pornography and had sex with him and when the senior pastor uses his "authority" to silence the boy. We use these words when we speak to a woman whose "shepherd" used counseling sessions to repeatedly rape her so she would learn what men like and so be a better wife. We use these words when a female comes alone before a board of all male "shepherds" with an accusation of rape or battering and ends up being cross-examined rather than believed. We are using familiar theological words and concepts in ways that sanction or minimize abuse and crush human beings. We assume we hold the correct position. Instead, we need to examine our individual and collective histories, our use of words, and our biases and prejudices that we have baptized with theological language.

A tree is known by its fruit. The fruit of the church ought never to use power to serve the self or to be complicit in such things. We need to listen to and learn from one another, just as I had to do when first hearing stories of abuse and violence that were unimaginable to me. That is incarnational work. We are failing our Lord and his body if we do not.

The Faces of Divorce

We have lost sight of the fact that our God hates divorces of all shapes and sizes, not just the termination of a legal relationship. Is it disunion to hide yourself every evening, looking at pornography behind a closed door, ignoring spouse and family? Is it a violation to batter a spouse whether with objects, fists, or words? Is it disunion to bar your spouse from any access to money? Is it divorce to pour out rage and humiliation on your family and deceitfully present a different face at church? Have you not, in the words of Malachi, broken faith with your spouse and acted both treacherously and deceitfully? God says, "I hate when a man covers his wife with violence, cruelty, and injustice. I hate the sending away" (Mal. 2:16). Don't all of the above involve a sending away? Where did we get the idea that the only thing we can call "divorce" is a piece of paper provided by the court? And how did we decide that all these other divorces do not mean anything significant as long as the paper from the court has not been delivered? Are we really sanctioning sin and destruction in a relationship intended to be a refuge for the sake of a legal document? If so, we are protecting the deformity of an entity that is meant to reflect Christ and his body.

We have misled many suffering people with our very narrow, limited interpretation of what God hates. We respond as if God hates the dissolution of a marriage but can tolerate abuse, harshness, manipulation, and threats in a relationship that is meant to look like his relationship to his bride! In doing so, we have contributed to the damage of precious people created in the image of God and confused them about who God is and what he says. We have also failed those who abuse by minimizing, excusing, and glossing over things God hates. We have valued the external appearance of marriage over the holiness of God lived out in hidden places.

Christendom's Teachings on Being Female

Much has been said throughout the centuries about what it means to be female. Men have said most of it. Women have been labeled the weaker sex, the second sex, the subordinate sex, and the devil's gateway. The church fathers had much to say about women. Here are a few examples:

Epiphanius: "In very truth, women are a feeble race."[1]

John Knox: "Weak, frail, impatient, feeble, inconstant, variable and lacking in the spirit of counsel."[2]

Aquinas: "Woman is defective and misbegotten."[3]

Augustine: "I do not see what sort of help woman was created to provide men with, if one excludes procreation."[4]

Chrysostom: "God maintained the order of each sex by dividing the business of life into two parts and assigned the more necessary and beneficial aspects to the man, and the less important, inferior matters to the woman."[5]

These comments and others made down through the centuries have contaminated our theological waters. They are lies. They are corrupt fruit and continue to reproduce in their own likeness. Women have been labeled unworthy, unclean, unintelligent, and insignificant. We have been called hysterical, silly, illogical, and unstable.

The commentary on what it means to be female is not replete with compliments or praise. Some of you know this is so because you have studied the topic. Many of you know because you have lived it. You have been labeled and discarded or set aside. Others have named you, identified and described you. As one named female, you are assumed to bear certain characteristics, to belong to a certain category, and to have specific qualities. To be called female is often to be demeaned and trashed—often in the house of God.

We have become accustomed to absorbing these views without much discernment. We have not examined but have sanctified what has been handed down to us. The damage and losses we have sustained are immeasurable. It is time to be quiet before God and acknowledge with humility that none of us has or will ever figure out the mind of God. We sound as if we think we know his mind and his thoughts. Our condemnations of those who think otherwise are harsh and often ugly. The arrogance is stunning. We all need to pause, listen, and reflect with a large dose of humility.

Ask yourself: What did I learn as a child about being male or female? What was explicitly taught? What was experientially taught? Did they match? What traditions regarding gender have been handed down through the generations of my family? What did I see going on relationally between male and female? Respect? Kindness? Rage? Labeling? Humiliation? Silence? What did I learn from advertising, music, and the internet about being male and female?

What did I learn from Christendom about being male and female? Through what words and what deeds was this taught? Did the words and the deeds match? Did the church teach that the male/female relationship is always hierarchical, never relational? How did the church respond to the gifts of women? How were women considered or encouraged? What gifts in women were nurtured beyond the "traditional" ways of viewing women? What theology was used to support the views I observed? Have I ever examined Scripture to see what I might learn? Have I ever studied deeply how our Lord interacted with females and what his ways teach us? Do his interactions turn any of the things I have believed on their head? (Hint: They should.) When God always agrees with us about any topic, we have created him in our image rather than bowing to his.

When I was thirteen, we attended a church that was very conservative. Somehow I got the message that girls with active brains were not welcome. So I developed a little fantasy for Sunday mornings. I imagined walking up the steep steps to the church doors and seeing a gray box on the ground (like an old-fashioned milk delivery box). I would pretend to take my brain out and put it carefully in the box to be picked up on my way out. I never told anyone about this image until I was an adult.

I am grieved I felt the need to imagine this. But I knew I could pick up my brain on the way out and that it was fully welcomed at home and at school. Many young girls have no safe or welcoming place for their brains. It saddens me when the church around the globe is not welcoming to the minds and gifts of females. In some places, it seems as if women have been amputated from the church.

When I held my newborn children and grandchildren, I felt as though I was looking at a treasure box packed intentionally by God with gifts to bless his world. Opening those gifts has been one of the great joys of my life. Ignoring the gifts of God in any child, female or male, does great damage to the child. It also greatly impairs the function of the church, because those gifts are given by God for the good of the body of Christ and for the glory of God.

How many sermons have you heard about women? I've listened to countless sermons over seven decades. Many have been excellent and have fed my soul. But I've never heard a sermon about Miriam, Huldah, Deborah, Phoebe, Priscilla, or Junia. I have heard sermons about Bathsheba, but they were not about David's gross abuse of power. He killed one of his sheep (Uriah) and required another man's wife to come to his bed. One does not say no to the king. King David was Bathsheba's Harvey Weinstein.[6] That abuse of power has rarely been spoken about from the pulpit.

Over twenty years ago, I taught a seminary class on women in the church. One of the requirements was to read selections from Ruth Tucker's book *Daughters of the Church*. Most of the students were young men, many of whom responded with openness. They had no knowledge of the history of women in the church and the gifts they generously bestowed on God's people (neither did the female students). Reading some of that history altered something for them; they talked about seeing and thinking about women differently. They saw them as thinkers, prophets, culture changers, and strong lovers of God. Those students developed a fuller picture of how God has gifted and called women.

Our starting point in thinking about men and women must be God's categories. Two humans were created by God, *both* in his image. He called them to the *same* work of bearing fruit, ruling, and subduing. They were called to sing a duet to the glory of God. *Both* humans fell by their own lust. *Both* followed a lie cloaked in a bit of truth. *Both* heeded a voice other than God's. *Both* received significant consequences from God. None of those consequences were part of God's original design. We seem to understand and fight against the consequences of the fall. We battle all but one: "And he shall rule over you." That one we have baptized and as a result have reaped a harvest of divisions, arguments, condemnation, and disdain.

We have allowed this discussion about the role of women to cause division in the body of Christ. I believe gender, God's design, and the fall are important areas of discussion, topics we need to continue to wrestle with in the light of Scripture *and* in the Spirit of Christ. I also believe that women have been hindered, in both secular and Christian society, from exercising their God-given gifts. The church has frequently failed to encourage women to use their minds, and women have been pressed into a particular, solitary mold of wife and mother and judged as ungodly, unworthy, inadequate, or unfeminine if they don't fit the mold. Some have not been called by God to that path. Others have been called to that path for a portion of their lives but not in their totality. The church is significantly poorer for clinging to its well-loved boxes, many of which are highly influenced by culture, the church fathers, and tradition.

The labels and categories of this debate have changed throughout my lifetime. They will change again. Today, one of the main questions seems to be "Are you complementarian or egalitarian?" Often hidden in that question is "I will approve of you if you choose the right label." These categories are not found anywhere in the Scriptures. In fact, the theological basis often used for maleness and femaleness is entirely out of line with the creeds and orthodoxy of Christianity throughout the centuries. The theological basis is the assertion that Jesus is eternally subordinate to the Father.[7] Many who adopted the categories for marriage have since criticized the theological basis, yet they still defend the categories as if they were part of the church's ancient creeds. It seems odd that we are teaching only two forms for marriage—complementarian and egalitarian—when our sublimely creative Father has not created all females or males alike. Surely the duets of such unions would also be unique. I will not settle this debate here, but this is something we have allowed to deeply divide the body of our Lord. We need to stand together rather than reducing our view of marriage to wherever men and women happen to be on the power grid.

In Acts we are told about a married couple whom Paul loved and worked with but who seem to fall outside the categories being discussed today. Priscilla and Aquila met Paul in Corinth, and the three of them worked and traveled together. Paul demonstrated confidence in them both by leaving *them* in charge of the church in *their* home (1 Cor. 16:19).

It was in Ephesus that Priscilla and Aquila met Apollos. When they heard him speaking in the synagogue, *they* took him aside and explained the way of God (theology) more clearly to him. Priscilla was clearly not just serving coffee or "supporting" Aquila. She is mentioned first in four out of five instances. Paul sanctioned *their* work in Ephesus and called *them* coworkers (Rom. 16:3). This from the pen of the same man who wrote, "Let a woman learn in silence with all submission" (1 Tim. 2:11

NKJV). Rather than triggering dueling Scriptures and more division, this tension should give us pause and put us on our knees in humility before God and with one another. It should also give rise to a question: Do you perhaps have a silenced Priscilla in your church?

Considering the ways in which God in the flesh interacted with women, a pause in this dialogue seems wise.[8] I suggest we lay down our weapons and seek our God. He hates the abuse of women and children; he hates demeaning, humiliating words toward any of his creatures. He hates that some in leadership have *in his name* denied, hidden, covered, and been complicit in abuses he says are worthy of a millstone. He grieves the damage to men and their loss of a yokefellow in all areas of life. Given that God hates these things and is grieved by them, I believe that repentance, humility, and seeking his face are the only right paths to pursue. What does this look like?

We all need to start with a willingness to see error in ourselves, something none of us likes to do. We're much more comfortable finding error in others, and we're good at it. Might we be willing to consider our assumptions, asking God for light and truth? Is it possible some have not come from Scripture at all but have been added to it? Surely we would all acknowledge our frailty, limitations, and lack of wisdom as creatures. We often make assumptions and then look at Scripture, which can easily be twisted to say all manner of things. We have done so with slavery, with females, and with males. We have done so in our responses to abuse and with so many aspects of our cultures. Having the humility to ask God to search us in these matters is good and right.

The process of learning a new language involves something called the silent period. You listen receptively to a previously unknown voice. It literally changes your mind and the way you think. If you are so arrogant that you can't think differently, you cannot learn a new language.[9] I have had to practice a silent

101

period in my work with trauma victims. They spoke a language I did not know and told stories I had never heard. I chose to push my thoughts, my categories, and my language aside and enter in until I learned something of what it was like to be them.

Does this sound familiar? It should. It is in essence an incarnation, learning what it is like to live in the flesh of another. We know someone who did this for us. Are we not to follow his example? Male pastors and leaders, have you ever asked women what it is like to be female in the church or organization you lead? Have you asked your wife and other women you know how they observe you using your power with them and in leadership and other relationships? Should women in leadership ask others the very same questions? Yes, absolutely.

Restoration of God's Governance

Let's go back to the beginning once again. Man was created first, and God declared man's aloneness "not good." God caused Adam to sleep and wounded him in order to create his bride. They were one flesh. God said a man is to leave home to join with his bride. Do you see the foreshadowing? Christ left the home of his Father. He put on flesh and became a servant, a helper for us. He lay down on the cross and was wounded and died to create his bride, the church. Adam was the head of the human race. Jesus is the Head of his church. Our Head is the Lamb slain from the foundation of the world (Rev. 13:8). He is power bending, power wounded for the sake of his bride. Headship is cruciform; it goes by way of the cross.

God created male and female in his image and gave them joint tasks (Gen. 1:26–28). They were to rule and subdue the earth and creation, not each other. They lived and worked together under the governance of God . . . until they did not. Deceived by God's archenemy, they acted outside the realm of God, and life was forever changed. In response, God spoke with them about the outcome of their choice. To Eve, he said in part, "Your desire will be for your husband, and he will *rule over you*" (3:16 NIV). We have lost sight of the fact that this is part of what we call the curse. This is *not* instruction for the man. It is a consequence of wrong and sinful choices.

Restoration of the governance of God is the remedy. Part of our call is to fight against the devastating, divisive, and destructive outcomes of a division of labor God did not ordain and to work to restore God's governance over male/female relationships, which ought to be the place of greatest beauty in displaying the image of our God.

Sadly, authoritarian treatment of females (and all church members) is often supported using the concept of headship. But we've lost sight of that concept. Abuse of any kind of power is clearly condemned in Ephesians: "Let no verbal abuse come out of your mouth, . . . no rage, no revenge, and no animosity. Be kind, be tender, and look like your God by walking sacrificially in your giving and your loving. . . . Live in the light, bearing the fruit of goodness, righteousness, and truth and exposing the deeds of darkness" (4:29, 31–32; 5:1–2). *Then* comes "the husband is *head* of the wife, *as also Christ* is head of the church; and He is the Savior of the body" (5:23 NKJV).

What does Christ look like as Head of the church and Savior of the body? He becomes little, bending down, touching sickness, protecting the vulnerable, washing feet, dying, and bearing pain *for* another, not causing pain *to* another. Humans flourish under such love. Being the Head means being the Servant of sinful, frail, confused, and broken human beings. Are not heads of things supposed to *have* servants, not *be* servants? But our Lord said, "The one who is the greatest among you must become like the youngest [the one with the least power], and the leader like the servant" (Luke 22:26). Likeness to Christ means inviting, not demanding. It means loving, not controlling. To be a head means to turn the curse upside down, not to rule over others. The Son of Man did not rule, though his disciples longed for him to do so. Instead, he held out his great arms and said, "Come. It is safe." He did not demand. He said, "Come and drink" (even if you are an immoral woman from the "wrong" race). Headship that follows Jesus is headship like no human ever conceived it to be. The head of a home, the head of a church is to be the greater servant. It is diabolical, even sacrilegious, that we send abused women home and leave abused children unprotected because someone is the "head"! To abuse power of any kind is to utterly fail to look like our Lord. To abuse or quash anyone in any way is to further the curse. Our God has called us to live so as to reverse the curse in any way we can. He calls us to go by way of the cross.

Our Head, while here in the flesh, demonstrated headship through an adolescent girl who brought him into the world. He demonstrated headship through a woman (an "unreliable source") who told people the Redeemer had come. He demonstrated headship through a formerly tormented woman who followed him everywhere. He chose her, a female with a problematic history, to tell his disciples that he had risen. Her voice still rings around this globe. We repeat her message every Easter. Do we encourage women to bring Jesus into our world, telling all that the Redeemer has come? Do we encourage women to use their voices to tell their brothers that Jesus is risen? Is there a Mary in your church? God help us if with our labels and categories we ignore or silence women around this globe who love him and have faith in him. We deprive his body of those prophetic voices, given by his authority, who pronounce that he is risen.

We must bring all our divisions involving male and female to our Lord, bowing to the governance of our God rather than expecting others to bow to ours. God says that in Christ earthly categories are null (Gal. 3:28). Instead, we are all to be clothed with Christ. That and that alone should be our dominant characteristic.

A man can bless a woman abundantly without even knowing it. A female client with a history of chronic and violent sexual abuse shared this story. She was afraid of men and of church, since that's where much of her abuse had occurred. After several years of counseling sessions with me, she wanted to go to church again. She attended every Sunday, sitting in the back, arriving late, and leaving early. After a few months, she told me about a family that sat in front of her every Sunday, a father, mother, and two little girls. She watched them like a hawk, most particularly the father. She said, "I have never seen a man treat a woman or little girls like this man does. He is never rough or sharp. Every Sunday, week after week, he is kind. He treats his wife with dignity. He bends down to the little girls, and even if they are wiggly or naughty, his voice is low and kind. For the first time in my life, I have a little picture of how you say God is with me. He is like that father."

This man demonstrated power under the control of the Spirit of God, manifested in humility and used on behalf of others. He demonstrated power with kindness. He looked like his Lord. He did not know that his humility carried tremendous power with eternal results, as he gave my client a glimpse of the Father as he truly is. Our Father, our Head, uses all power to bless his children as he bends over them with love and serves them. That very God, in Christ, calls us to do the same.

eight

The Intersection of Race and Power

Deep within the darkness of a womb, a little one is being carefully, lovingly knit together by our Father's hands. The child is a gift created in his likeness, intended to bring him glory and bless his world and its inhabitants. When he has finished knitting, the Father wraps this tiny gift in beautiful black skin, and she enters the world. Grievously, as she will discover, not everyone in her world sees her as her Father does. James Baldwin says in *Notes of a Native Son*, "Black is a terrible color with which to be born into this world."[1] Baldwin's observation tells us that something has gone horribly wrong in our world. The statement reflects a message that many have received from both secular and Christian culture, a message the author heard in surround sound. Baldwin's experience in this world made the Father's love appear to be a lie, his gift devalued. Lies about our Father, whether taught by word or deed, are diabolical. And many of those lies have been taught and internalized.

It's striking to note how hostile the conversation can get when considering issues of race and the abuse of power. Sadly, this is no less true in Christendom than elsewhere. Name-calling, labeling, and demeaning language are used as weapons. Someone tells the story of their experience, and they are quickly accused of falsehood, victimhood, socialism, un-Christian beliefs, and weakness for not "getting over it." Let me be clear: there is no excuse for believers in Christ to speak this way to one another—or to nonbelievers—no matter the topic.

Any encounter with another human being needs to be grounded in two foundational truths. We've already hinted at the first. You will never meet, talk to, walk with, or work beside a human being who has not been purposefully knit together by the hands of our Father. Never. Everyone designed by our Father is precious, and he calls us to treat each other as such—as members of the human race, created by our God and dearly loved. We are all one race, the human race, and in that race, all are image bearers. There are no exceptions. In Acts, Paul says, "[God] made *from one man* every nation of mankind to live on all the face of the earth. . . . For in him we live and move and have our being. . . . We are indeed his offspring" (17:26, 28 ESV). Jonathan Blanchard, the first president of Wheaton College as well as an abolitionist, coined the phrase "one-bloodism" in reference to this Scripture passage.[2] You will never meet a human being with whom you do not share the blood of Adam.

The second foundational truth is rooted in the incarnation and tells us how to walk with and live with one another. "And the Word became flesh and dwelt among us, and we beheld His glory . . . full of grace and truth" (John 1:14 NKJV). We are *always* to walk as Christ did. To treat anyone as less than is to defy the Father's judgment about who they are, violating the first truth. To treat others as less than is also to fail to look like Jesus in this world, violating the second truth. If we want to understand others, we must do as he did. He put on our flesh and entered our world, becoming like us and experiencing what our lives are like. In doing so, he became the hope of our salvation. But his life was also the greatest act of listening and of entering into the world of another that has ever been. He has called us to follow him in his ways.

Issues around race have set up and toppled kingdoms. They've led to fences and ovens and deportation and slavery. We have used the beautiful diversity our God created as a tool to gain power and oppress. The fruit of these actions is corrupt, life destroying, and demonic. Many long for this to change so the world can witness Christ followers who are full of grace and truth rather than disdain and division. I'm no expert on these issues. But I have spent decades wading through the rubble caused by injustice, hatred, the abuse of power, and generational trauma. It is a path of great pain, one that breaks the heart of our Father.

Look honestly at history. We have participated in the rejection and contempt of others based on race. The dignity, humanity, and value of one created in the image of God had to be denied or minimized in order for slavery to survive for more than two centuries in America. It does not take much thought to realize that damage was also done to slaveholders and to those silently complicit as well.

Consider the story of *Celia, a Slave.*[3] Celia was purchased by Robert Newsom at the age of fourteen. Newsom's purpose in buying her was not so she could be a field hand or a domestic servant. He wanted a replacement for his dead wife in the marital bed. Newsom was sixty years old. He deceivingly presented her as a servant for his daughters. She was, in fact, a slave and a concubine. If you have read about slavery in the United States, you know that rape was almost always part of the narrative for female slaves. All women were relatively powerless in the South. But a young female who was black and also a slave was triply vulnerable. Rape was against the law, but that law applied only to white females. Celia was raped for five years.

Celia had two children by Newsom and became pregnant with a third. She tried to get Newsom to stop raping her. He refused. So she hit him with a large stick and accidentally killed him. She burned his body in her fireplace, hoping to hide what had happened, but she was brought to trial before a jury of twelve white men. Her defense was considered radical because if extenuating circumstances were factored in, it would pose a great threat to slaveholders. The institution of slavery was, however, protected. She was found guilty and hanged on December 21, 1855. This happened in the same country that had declared less than a century prior, "All men are created equal and endowed by their Creator with certain inalienable rights—life, liberty, and the pursuit of happiness." Clearly, there were exceptions to that grand pronouncement. At that time, all the laws favored white males; they were the only ones with the power to create them, enforce them, or change them. Slaves had no recourse and no power.

What do you think Robert Newsom was doing to his own soul by owning humans as if they were chattel, raping at will, and destroying the life of an adolescent girl? What damage did he do to Celia? She was crushed, oppressed, raped, powerless, and voiceless. She was treated as a thing to be used by her master as he willed. His abuse of power is stunning. What damage was done to her three children, who were left motherless? How did they carry the story and its outcome? Did what happened to their mother escalate their fear as slaves? Did it harden their hearts? How do you suppose the children of the woman who murdered the master were treated by others?

I know stories about my family from much further back than 1855, when Celia was hanged. Those stories have shaped me. I have told them to my children and grandchildren. I suspect many of you could say the same. The story of Celia from 165 years ago is out there somewhere today, passed on to new generations and still bearing fruit.

In the early 1950s, I was four or five years old when my family drove from Virginia to Florida to visit my father's grandmother. We drove all night. Christine came with us. She was our maid and babysitter. She was black, and I adored her. My brother and I slept during the night with our heads in her lap while my parents took turns driving. In the morning, we pulled up to a restaurant. I looked out the window and saw two water fountains. A sign above one said, "Whites Only." Above the other, "Colored Only." I asked what that meant; Christine told me. My mother left us in the car and went into the restaurant. She returned, weeping, got in the car, and said insistently to my father, "Drive!" Now, my father rarely got angry, but when he did, you could tell because the right side of his mouth would turn down. He nodded to my mother, his mouth turned down, and we left. Why? Because the restaurant would not serve Christine. My parents were angry and heartbroken and refused to give the owners their business. We went without breakfast as we drove through the South. This was eighty years after emancipation.

If such an experience profoundly affected me, and it did, what do you think such repeated experiences have done through the years to those to whom the "Colored Only" sign referred? Why were subsequent protests necessary in order for image bearers to be granted the right to sit at a table or ride a bus? Many of those rejected will share the heavenly table spread for us by our God. Are we not to look like him now?

The Abuse of Power and Generational Trauma

Do we really think we can enslave millions of people for more than two hundred years, treating them as things to be used, crushing, oppressing, and humiliating them, without long-term effects reverberating throughout generations descended from both slaves and slaveholders? And we know the trauma and abuse did not stop with slavery. While about four million enslaved people in the United States were freed in 1863, our nation proceeded to crush African Americans with Jim Crow laws. Many fled north. In Isabel Wilkerson's excellent book *The Warmth of Other Suns: The Epic Story of America's Great Migration*, we read, "Blacks, though native born, were arriving as the poorest people, from the poorest section of the country, with the least access to the worst education."[4] Read it again; let it sink in. My hope is that we will see more clearly the overwhelming results of trauma echoing down through the centuries.

Trauma is a wound to personhood, to the self—a deep wound with a profound impact. Trauma shapes us. We have been created in the image of a God who speaks, relates, and has power. Trauma silences, isolates, and renders powerless. That which mars God's image is not of God. This fact is very important to me as a clinician. The people I see, like all of us, are easily shaped. So what happens when children, the most malleable of humans, are repeatedly imprinted with evil?

I suspect most of us have some awareness of our family histories. There are some exceptions, and the blankness of that space carries its own wounds. Some of us have family stories that instill dignity and pride. Others carry family stories like a burden, heavy with shame and sadness. It is likely that most of us have some of both. We have all been shaped by what has been passed down through generations.

The concept of concentration-camp syndrome or survivor syndrome emerged in the 1960s, noticed and then labeled by clinicians in Canada who were seeing the children of Holocaust survivors seeking mental health treatment. Further down the line, the grandchildren of those survivors were overrepresented by 300 percent in referrals as compared to the general population. At first the children were described as having secondary trauma, but when the same symptoms were evident in the third generation, we began to recognize what is now called the intergenerational transmission of trauma.[5] The phrase refers to trauma that occurred several generations ago and its impact on each new generation, psychologically, neurobiologically, and culturally. Behavioral and emotional responses to past trauma continue to shape the experiences of the present generation.

We can see, if we will just look, the tragic suffering and evil that result when humans are traumatized. We once thought of trauma as an event resulting in distressed humans showing certain symptoms. That can certainly still be true. We now recognize, however, that trauma can be a multifaceted, enduring part of life resulting in long-term damage to body, mind, heart, and soul. It is crucial in our desire to relieve suffering and speak truth that we have some understanding of the nature of trauma and its effects as well as how the transmission of generational trauma works so that our dialogues and our care of others are based on some grasp of that reality. We tend to minimize or dismiss such damage to make it feel more manageable to us.

A person is altered and shaped by chronic, complex trauma and oppression. The impact is mistrust, hopelessness, shame, and inferiority, with no sense of ability or choice. This person has no sense of self or identity (this is who I choose to be) and no integrity of the self. They are isolated, with no experience of love, no safety in relationships, and no sense of purpose except perhaps survival. Despair, hopelessness, and lack of purpose are predominant. You can take an adult with a relatively healthy childhood and an intact self and throw them into an Auschwitz, a Pitesti Prison, or a Tuol Sleng. You can put them on a ship, drag them away from home, and enslave them; or you can remove them from their land, take their children, and destroy all they hold dear, so traumatizing them that their former identities and structures of self are dismantled and crushed. They cannot recover from such events in a year or so. These experiences have been woven into them and have shaped their "I am." An entirely different person now hands down to future generations what has been burned into their soul. Talk about power. Both the individual story and the story of the people group get told over and over. Those stories, like the original events of which they tell, continue to shape future generations.

Restoration of Beauty

With those stories in mind, think of a favorite painting that is beautiful and worth a great deal of money. Maybe it's in a museum or a private collection. Perhaps it is a Rembrandt or a van Gogh. Whenever there is news about damage done to such a painting, people around the world respond with distress. A beautiful masterpiece created by an artist who is gone. A treasure mutilated and treated as if it had no value. Some who love art weep at such news. Every human being is one of God's masterpieces. No two are alike, each one is unique, but all are created by the same Artist. All are treasured by him and meant to bless others. All are signed with his name, coming directly from his hand. They carry the Master's image. They are gifts of beauty for all to see and enjoy. Destruction of such beauty is tragic. When we oppress, enslave, keep under, silence, demean, eliminate, or ostracize other human beings, we are trashing the exquisite artwork of our God.

Listen to God speak: "You who have authority, who abhor justice and make crooked all that is right . . . who build with bloodshed and unrighteousness . . . your leaders work for money . . . yet they say, 'Is not the LORD among us?'" (Mic. 3:9–11). Is this not a description of slavery? Was not slavery "sanctioned" by such passages? What about lynching, that grisly, public spectacle of dehumanization by which people were killed and soul damage was done to their families and to all African Americans? It was also destructive to those doing the lynching, the crowds who came to watch, and the powers that sanctioned such devastation. Does the passage not also describe the treatment of Indigenous peoples, the internment of Japanese Americans, the genocides and many other atrocities around the world? Do we not see that we are destroying not only humans created by God but also ourselves when we use power to engage in such evils, actively or passively? If we do not face the truth and truly repent, we will have to harden ourselves and repeatedly call evil good, passing such lies down to future generations. The stench of death is still with us.

Can you imagine the weeping our God has done and continues to do as across the centuries we have destroyed masterpieces of his creation? We as his people need to learn to watch with him, to weep with him. When we do this, in the words of a genocide survivor in Rwanda who lived through unspeakable atrocities and trauma, here is what happens: "I saw only evil. I no longer believed God to be good. The church was not a sanctuary for my family; it was a cemetery. But then you came, you listened, and you heard my broken heart. And now I think I can believe that God too is listening and hears my pain and will be my sanctuary because I have gotten a taste of him through you." This is what it looks like to use power, in the midst of atrocity, to bless others.

We can only bless this way when we view humans as God does. God became flesh and has shown us what is good. "And what does he require of us but to do justly, love mercy, and walk humbly with the Servant of Man" (Mic. 6:8). The fragrance of the Servant is the only antidote to the stench of death.

Healing Generational Trauma

God created humans in his image and blessed them abundantly so they in turn might transmit those blessings to succeeding

115

generations, multiplying the likeness of God everywhere. But when the first humans ate from the tree that marked the limitations of their freedom under God's governance, their ability to pass on blessings was marred.

We humans continue to pass down to others, but as we know, often what we pass down is not blessing but disease and ruin and trauma. Generational trauma is real and alive because the mechanism for blessing has so frequently been used to transmit sorrow, destruction, and evil. When we do have blessings to pass along, we too often refuse to share them with those we deem unlike us. We hurt them, and ourselves, by our refusal to bear God's image in this way.

Thankfully, Scripture is replete with references to God responding to ruin with the promise of blessing. In Genesis 12, after creation was marred and humans were no longer passing down the blessings of God to others, God said to Abram, "Leave your country, your relatives, and your place of origin. Leave all that is familiar to you. Leave home and live under my governance alone. I will make you a great nation and bless you . . . and in you *all* the families of the earth will be blessed" (vv. 1–3). God promised to pour out his blessings in abundance through the generations *to all nations*—even after humans had sinned—if they would live under his governance. In Isaiah 61:4, God promises, "They will rebuild the ancient ruins . . . raise up the former devastations; repair . . . the desolations of many generations" (NASB). This promise follows a description of Christ, who came for the poor, the brokenhearted, the incarcerated, and the enslaved. In coming to "them," he rebuilt ruins and healed generations. In Zechariah 8:4–5, we read, "Old men and old women will sit in the streets of Jerusalem . . . and the city streets will be filled with boys and girls playing there." The most vulnerable—the elderly and the young—will be safe in the streets. God will restore a place of safety and laughter and blessing for all. No exceptions. Bearing God's image means responding to ruin where we find it and pouring out blessing in that place so that it can be transformed.

I hope that we will be encouraged by recognizing that bit by bit, as we invest in even one life, trauma ceases to govern and hope springs up. God will take that bit of healing and bless future generations with it. That is an abundant outcome—beyond our ability to comprehend. He can and will rebuild ancient human ruins through us, piece by piece, as we become like him and participate in his work with him.

Sitting with Trauma

One of the first women I saw in my clinical practice was brought weekly by her pastor's wife, who recognized a wounded soul and did not know what to do. Neither did I. She came faithfully, sat in a chair in my office, and did not say a word for six months. I talked way too much at the beginning and eventually learned just to be quiet and be "with" her. When I later learned her story, I realized that those six months were her first experience of being with another human being and feeling safe. It was an immeasurable gift I did not know I was giving.

She was my teacher. She taught me how to leave my world and enter hers. She taught me how to listen so as to truly understand. She taught me how to sit with the horrors of her life so that she did not have to sit with them alone. She taught me not to script the healing of a human being. She eventually learned that God truly did love her and hated what had been done to her. She learned those things because I cared for her and hated what had been done. Oh, my mistakes were many for sure, but I stayed and listened and treated her with dignity and care. Ultimately, she taught me about Jesus and something of what it means to look like him to others. He became like us so that we could become like him. God used a very broken human being in redemptive ways in my life at least as much as he used my life for her.

Have you ever sat with someone unlike you, being grace and truth to them? Have you ever listened, trying to understand what it is like to be them rather than trying to correct them and make them like you? So often we listen just long enough to convince another to be more like us or to instruct them about how to "get over" whatever has happened. It is an egocentric approach. Jesus's presence with us was not and is not like that. He listened and responded to the individual. Have you ever been struck by the fact that he healed all blind people in unique ways? Let us watch Jesus and see who he was with others who were utterly unlike him. Let us watch and see who he was with "them."

Jesus and the Other

She was an outcast woman, rejected by many and considered less than. We spoke of her earlier. She was a Samaritan and therefore considered racially inferior. The Samaritans were a people of mixed race, and the Jews despised them more than "pure" gentiles because they saw Samaritans as polluting the blood of their forefathers.

No decent Jew of that day would have passed through Samaria, where "they" lived. But the pursuing God went into territory that was considered polluted to meet with a polluted woman he would have been expected to avoid, reject, and condemn. He chose the road others would not deign to take in protest of their reasons for avoiding it—their prejudice and pride. In doing so, he was pursuing the self-righteous as well, teaching them about who God is. He crossed over every obstacle to get to her. He let nothing stand in his way—not custom, prejudice, belief, honor, or appearances. He went to find her and, through her, the people of Samaria.

How did he begin his pursuit? By expressing his own need. The God who created the springs of the earth, the seas, and the rivers asked for water. He was weary and thirsty, and he brought his need, his vulnerability, to this "polluted" woman. "Help me. Give me a drink," he said. He drank water from her cup! He was the Word made flesh. In becoming thirsty, like her, he gained admission to her soul and to an entire village of "them."

Think about a group or individual you have categorized as "them." Is it possible that God is using their life and their voice to teach you more about himself? We as God's people need to ask others unlike ourselves, "Teach me what it is like to be you." We should be humbled in the presence of many who love Jesus in spite of a long history of prejudice and evil, often done in his name and with a twisting of his words. Our work is to listen, learn from, grieve with, walk with, and be changed to look more like our Lord. Talk about blessing! Jesus humbled himself and became obedient to death. If he would do that for us, perhaps we who name his name should humble ourselves and bow to the death of our assumptions, our prejudices, our distance, our arrogance, and our love of power. To fail to do so is to fail him.

God Blesses the Nations

If we are to be like the God who lived among us, we must understand and be governed by his view of the "other." First, *we* are the "other." We were nothing like him. He crossed innumerable barriers to come and live among us. He did not demand we cross over to find him. He knew we could not. He not only came to us but also went to the cross to become the bridge we needed to reach eternal life and healing. How unlike us. We do not want to cross barriers, and we prefer walls to bridges. He literally laid down his life so that we might know him and be like him in his world. That is what it means to live under the governance of God.

Second, he is the Creator God, and he obviously loves variety. Anyone who loves birds, flowers, and trees enjoys the diversity of beauty within those categories. Watching a bluebird, cardinal, goldfinch, and woodpecker simultaneously appear at my feeders brings a shot of joy. A diversity of musicians and instruments in a music ensemble is part of its beauty. Who can imagine Handel's *Messiah* without the harpsichord, or the trumpet, or the voices? God did not stop with nature or music. He created and continues to create a variety of humans. Look at the body of Christ—arms and legs and eyes and ears. All different and essential. All created purposefully. All demonstrating his glory and who he is. He is the three-in-one God. Demeaning variety and holding others in contempt are utterly against the God who made us. We dare not deprive God of the beautiful symphony of colors and gifts and untold differences that he created. When we refuse his governance, we fail to follow the Composer, and we damage the Master's work. We are to find joy and beauty and to bestow dignity in humans of all kinds, from all nations, in all stations of life.

Finally, God's love of and joy in the beautiful array of humanity is seen in the nations, in the ethnicities. There are not only diverse individuals but also diverse nations. Go back to Abram in Genesis 12, where he is told by God to leave everything. Put yourself under my governance, God says, and "in you *all* the families of the earth will be blessed" (v. 3 NASB). He says *all*, everyone. God was blessing every ethnicity, every tribe, and every nation through Abram. There were no exceptions. Are we not to look like him?

Every time we treat someone with dignity rather than shame, respect rather than disregard, concern rather than exploitation, kindness rather than brutality, and careful attention rather than turning away, we are doing things that are the reverse of trauma and evil.[6]

God will restore a place of safety and laughter and blessing. In the meantime, he has called us to do the same for one another. Have we actively worked to repair the desolations of generations? Or do we say, "I was not there. It is over. You should be fine now." Do we spend our efforts to ensure safe streets for the vulnerable in our towns and cities? Or do we let "them" live wherever they live and feel grateful we live elsewhere? Has our presence as the body of Christ in this world blessed the nations, both around the world and at our door?

The blessing of God on the nations was evident for all to see at Pentecost. We are told that people were there from every nation under heaven, beautiful variety brought together by the Spirit of our God to hear of his wonderful works. God intentionally made certain that all the nations could understand in an intimate way. He also ensured that all the nations were there together hearing the same truth. We, the body of Christ, have been called and given power to share the same truth in our day. We are to make God known to everyone by words and deeds, anticipating the final great unity of all people, nations, and tribes gathered around the throne of the Lamb.

nine

Power Abused in the Church

On several occasions, I have traveled to Rwanda, where in 1994 close to a million people were systematically slaughtered in a genocide that lasted one hundred days. The world did nothing. Worse, many churches in Rwanda were complicit in the genocide. Many people fled into the churches for sanctuary and instead were massacred within the church's walls. Today, several churches around the country stand untouched as a memorial to what happened. You can go into these churches, where sunlight comes through broken stained glass and the bones of thousands lie just as they died, 2,500 in one, 4,000 in another, and on it goes. Hell came not only to Rwanda but also to the church. One woman said to me, "The churches were the ground of the genocide." A young man said, "I used to think of the church as a sanctuary, but now I think of it as a cemetery." The sanctuary of the Life Giver became the place of death with the assistance of his people and their shepherds.

How can such a thing be? How do the people of God become ministers of death? How is it that those who claim to follow the Crucified One can take up machetes against neighbors and friends or turn them over to be slaughtered by others? How is it that a church that named the name of Jesus can have an open Bible on its bloody altar and be filled with the skeletons of those who died hideous deaths in the place of hoped-for sanctuary? How can shepherds of the sheep prove to be wolves who devour? How can those who say they are Christians slaughter people in a very close, face-to-face way in the house of the God they say they worship? Did they not know that the Word of God forbids such a thing? Did they not know that God was weeping? Surely they did. Did that not matter?

The answer is terribly complex. I do not pretend to be able to plumb its depths. I have pieces of knowledge that help me but certainly not enough to truly explain such a thing. I know that colonialism leaves countries weakened, without infrastructure and ripe for dictators and civil wars and corruption. I know that grinding poverty and a lack of education make people desperate and willing to follow almost anyone who says they can make things better. And I know something of the human heart, which is "more deceitful than all else and is desperately sick" (Jer. 17:9 NASB). The heart lies to itself and others and tends to lead us astray from right precepts. But how does one's heart get *that* far astray?

One of the meanings of the word *deceitful* is "foot-tracked." The term pertains to detectable evidence of a visible track of a substance. I grew up around hunters. They are on the lookout for detectable evidence of a visible track. They see it in the rubbings of buck in the woods, in footprints, in droppings. If we look carefully, we will see that over time a deceived heart leaves tracks. To understand what happened in Rwanda, we must go back to find the trail of evidence that helps to explain the outcome.

A heart does not become genocidal overnight. It does, however, leave evidence on its trail. Genocide begins when people gain facility in doing a mean or heartless thing to a fellow human. Genocide begins when people malign their brothers and sisters more easily today than yesterday. Genocide begins when people travel the crooked way more freely. When the poison ceases to sicken them, then their hearts are desperately wicked. When the sting no longer wounds and the conscience ceases to upbraid, they have allowed iniquity to abound. Such things are the detectable evidence of a visible track of sin. They can result in genocide. Do we see that if sin abounds in our hearts as individuals and as a corporate body, we end up killing ourselves and others?

There is evidence of tracks in the lives of those who abuse children or are complicit with such perpetrating. If we look, we will see evidence of tracks in the lives of those clergy who feed on their sheep. Such things result in smaller "genocides." These acts are not the slaughter of a people, but they do bring death to human beings, death to dignity, to hope, to trust, and to faith. Sin, we are told, brings forth death. Such acts emerge little by little. The result in Rwanda was a visible, heart-wrenching picture of what happens when shepherds meant to shelter and feed their flocks instead become predatory themselves or complicit with predators. Sadly, the churches of Rwanda offer a clear view of what has and is happening in many faith communities today in this country and around the world.

I have been working with abuses of many kinds for more than four decades. That work has been with people *in* the Christian community. When I see victims of sexual or domestic abuse, clergy sexual abuse, rape, and spiritual abuse, I am working with those who name the name of Christ. And when I work with perpetrators or hear about them, I am working with or hearing about those who name the name of Christ. The majority of abusers, and their supporters, have consistently used theological teachings to cover up abuse, or excuse it, or return the victim to the abuser. Such a stunning response ignores the fact that abuse damages victims and perpetrators alike. It damages families, often for generations. It damages church communities, mission boards, and Christian organizations. It damages precious people created in the image of our God.

We've all seen the news. Power in God's house has been abused in God's name by notorious pastors and leaders who have been sexually involved with multiple sheep, who have used money fraudulently, who have been verbally nasty and demeaning and controlling of others. Or they have known about and been complicit in the cover-up "for the sake of the church."

The headlines are cause for grief because we have seen that abuse in the church is not something that happens only to "other" groups or some category of "them." Abuse and subsequent cover-ups are a widespread problem in congregations of all sizes and denominations. The light has been turned on in the church, and we are being called by God to wrestle with what ought not to be. It is crucial that we pay attention and understand the issues involved in order to protect God's sheep, proactively train shepherds who will not damage the sheep of God, and wisely come alongside those who have been victims of abuse in God's family. If we do not, we will hear the words God spoke to the shepherds of Israel who fed themselves rather than their sheep: "Those who are sickly you have not strengthened, the diseased you have not healed, the broken you have not bound up, the scattered you have not brought back, nor have you sought for the lost; but with force and with severity you have dominated them" (Ezek. 34:4 NASB). Because the shepherds misused their God-given power, failed to care for wounded sheep, and allowed the flock of Israel to become prey, God removed the flock from their care.

Spiritual Abuse

Here are two words that should never go together: *spiritual* and *abuse*. It's a diabolical pairing. The Spirit of God hates abuse, uncovers abuse, and cares for the abused. But we often see spirituality being misused to damage a person created in the image of God. Spiritual abuse involves using the sacred to harm or deceive the soul of another.

What power tools might someone use to carry out such diabolical work? They're the tools common in every kind of abuse. The most obvious is words. When we use God's sacred Word in a way that harms another, commanding them to do wrong, manipulating them, deceiving them, or humiliating them, we have spiritually abused them. We tell them, "God says," but we don't reflect the character of the God whose words we use. We twist God's words in order to coerce, to manipulate.

A powerful position in a religious context carries inherent spiritual authority. Pastor, priest, elder, Christian school teacher, and youth leader are all positions that invite trust. Their spiritual authority lends credence to words spoken claiming to accurately represent God. A certain character is assumed when, in fact, position may be used to hide character. Remember, Jesus's strongest rebukes were for those religious leaders who used the words of God to crush and control.

A pastor with a theological degree and knowledge of Scripture can lift words out of those Scriptures, pronounce them with authority, and wound those under their care. An ability to articulate theological truths does *not* mean the speaker is an obedient servant of God. A spiritual leader has all the power tools at their disposal and can use them to harm verbally, sexually, emotionally, physically, financially, and spiritually. No matter the tool or the method of delivery, all forms of abuse always do spiritual damage. One cannot sexually, physically, or verbally abuse another person without also inflicting spiritual abuse.

Spiritual Leadership

Edwin Friedman, in his 1985 book *Generation to Generation*, writes about two qualities of leadership that our culture demands: expertise and charisma.[1] Sadly, many of us in Christendom have looked for those same qualities in our leaders. The demand for expertise often forces leaders to be defined in terms of their abilities. A good leader will be an expert, perpetually acquiring more information and demonstrating an ever-increasing proficiency. A pastor, then, is one who demonstrates expertise in theology, teaching, preaching, counseling, budget planning, administration, mediating, and social relationships. A leader is expected to know more, achieve more, and perform better. The more adequate they are in those areas, the more they are declared a success. Leadership is thus reduced to a never-ending treadmill of acquiring more and better skills and achieving impressive results. Balance budgets, increase membership, deliver interesting and inspirational sermons, offer quick fixes in counseling, and run an efficient and organized ministry.

According to Friedman, charisma—that strongly attractive personality exuded by certain people—is the second leadership quality our culture demands. Charismatic leaders can unify divided bodies, build enthusiasm, and galvanize people to action; they can help people feel optimistic by sending a message that things are going in a good direction.

Meeting the expectations of expertise and charisma puts tremendous pressure on a leader. Groups who follow such leaders assume that if success is not forthcoming, the leader is to blame. Naturally, when hoped-for results don't become a reality, the leader generally responds by trying harder, hiding anything that threatens a reputation for success.

When a leader's powerful presence coincides with a growing church, a global influence, an influential media presence, and a steady inflow of money, their followers believe that the leader is the one who has made it all happen. It follows that any attack on or criticism of that leader will not be believed or must be denied. A threat to the leader is a threat to all.

Given this dynamic, it's easy to see how leaders in the church allow themselves to be governed by the outward results of their service. When the demands are great and the pressure is on, leaders can be seduced into fealty to the ministry and equate that with obedience to Christ. Decisions are driven by what will succeed or bring in money or produce greater numbers. Such things are not inherently bad, but when they become the main things, they become devastatingly destructive. It's tempting to worship the work. But the call to ministry is not a call to love and obedience to the work and its demands but a call to Jesus Christ alone. In Luke 10:20, Jesus sends seventy workers out ahead of him; they come back spouting the marvelous outcomes they've achieved. "Don't rejoice in your successful service," Jesus tells them. "Rejoice in knowing me." When ministry outcomes come to govern the work, tremendous anxiety results—anxiety about sustaining success, anxiety about being discovered a fraud, anxiety that someone else is doing it better. Leaders are often driven to do whatever it takes to make themselves feel better, even if that means using people, substances, or illicit behaviors to alleviate the ever-present anxiety.

Character, Personal History, and Accountability of Leaders

Though rarely spoken about, character and personal history are shaping influences in those who lead. We frequently select leaders according to their gifts rather than their character. Leadership in the body of Christ should be based not on natural abilities but on spiritual maturity and Christlikeness. We've seen some very immature leaders in the Christian world rise to power because of their gifts rather than spiritual maturity. We should never assume that verbal gifts and theological acumen are accompanied by maturity and integrity of character. This bears repeating: the ability to articulate theological truths does not necessarily mean that one is an obedient servant of God. Unfortunately, the abilities and knowledge that bring ministry success easily become ego food.

The work of the church is not the call to ministry. Our true work is that of manifesting likeness to Christ in all things, whether in success or failure, criticism or praise. If numbers, growth, and fame were God's measures, then Jesus would be deemed a failure. Likeness to Christ is not measured by such external things but by the extent to which a person's character bears fruit that resembles the fruit of the Spirit. Not by numbers but by kindness. Not by fame but by humility and self-control.

Many pastors have never really thought through how their personal history has shaped them and therefore shaped their ministries. A young boy can grow up under an abusive, alcoholic father who demeans him and beats him. Then, without looking at the impact of that, he can settle into ministry and a pulpit, a position of power. He may be bright and verbally gifted and gain success. However, his ability to handle criticism, his defensiveness, and his difficulty with intimacy, coupled with a fear of failure born of his father's rage, will make him extremely vulnerable. Any correction or criticism will be highly threatening.

Character work and an understanding of one's personal history are not usually emphasized in training for ministry. This is unwise given our heart's capacity for deception. I have found that many young church leaders grew up unchurched, came to Christ in college, headed for seminary (maybe), and then landed in a pulpit with little to no supervision. Some come from homes full of rage, alcoholism, promiscuity, pornography, or drugs and may have their own histories in these areas. Others come from homes full of the knowledge of God, but the emphasis has been on being right or demonstrating "spiritual" success.

The pride and arrogance underlying such attitudes are never considered until somewhere down the road when they leak out in destructive ways.

We're in too much of a hurry to value Moses's forty years in the desert, Abraham's decades of waiting, Jesus's forty days in the wilderness, and Paul's years of solitude in the desert and then in Tarsus. None of these leaders started without an extended time of aloneness with God. None of these shepherds rode in on a white horse promising success and growth—not even our Lord. Yet we seem hungry for our leaders to produce positive outcomes, feelings, and experiences and to gain the favor of as many people as possible. Our world needs those with spiritual influence to truly know the Good Shepherd. He knew how to tend, feed, and protect his flock. He also knew what it was like to be one of those lambs, because he became one when he took on flesh and lived among us (not above us).

Pastors and leaders often live with little to no oversight. I cannot tell you how many pastors, young and old, have shared with me, often with tears, their longings for good mentors. They long for someone to listen and ask hard questions. They are eager to be taught about faithful ministry and about integrity in ministry and in the home. They have no one in their lives for whom they are not also responsible as a shepherd.

All these factors can work together to make ministry a dangerous place for pastors and hence for their sheep. I believe the church needs to give serious consideration to the ramifications of our failure to grasp these truths. When soil repeatedly produces a bad crop, it is foolish to be angry with the plants. The soil needs to be examined and clearly needs a serious overhaul. We need to think wisely about what it means to shepherd and what *God's* requirements are to be a good one. Character has supremacy in the kingdom of God. It is character that bears fruit in this world, and that fruit is full of the fragrance of Christ, in all his humility.

Power in a Spiritual Context

Research on power and compassion/empathy has shown that elevated social power is associated with a diminished reciprocal emotional response to another's sufferings.[2] In other words, the more power a person holds in relation to other people, the less empathy they will have. That's very troubling in any context. In a spiritual setting such as a church, it is frightening. A lack of compassion is diametrically opposed to the calling of God.

People considered to have high power in an organization or other group setting tend to have certain characteristics, according to one research study.[3] Imagine these qualities in someone who is a pastor or a teacher:

- feel fewer social restraints
- judge others' emotions less accurately
- react less to others' emotions
- do not adjust their demands to another's emotion
- experience less distress with talker's distress level
- stereotype others more
- are more resource rich
- are aware they can act at will without interference or serious social consequences
- exhibit disinhibited, self-serving behavior, which increases the likelihood of socially inappropriate behaviors

If a real-life shepherd tending four-legged sheep functioned this way, their sheep would all die. The shepherd is smarter, can do what they want, and does not respond to distress in the sheep. They may in fact think the sheep are "just a bunch of dumb sheep." The sheep are utterly vulnerable.

In contrast, here are some characteristics of low-power people:

- experience greater social restraints, threats, or punishments
- assimilate more to high-power person's emotions
- concede more to anger than to happiness in high-power persons
- exhibit an increase in distress in response to high-power person's distress
- are more likely to be vulnerable to aggression and bullying
- are more likely to be female or of a different race than those in power
- attend to others more carefully and are vigilant so as to navigate threatening social environments
- inhibit the direct expression of their own ideas[4]

The vulnerability of low-power people is glaringly obvious. If we take these results and observations from the research and put them into a spiritual context where the Word of God is frequently invoked by those with power, we see that the potential for abuse in God's name is quite stunning. The house of God, meant to be a refuge for the people of God, is in fact not safe. Listen to the prophet Ezekiel:

> Therefore, you shepherds, hear the word of the LORD: As surely as I live, declares the Sovereign LORD, because my flock lacks a shepherd and so has been plundered and has become food for all the wild animals, and because my shepherds did not search for my flock but cared for themselves rather than for my flock, therefore, you shepherds, hear the word of the LORD: This is what the Sovereign LORD says: I am against the shepherds and will hold them accountable for my flock. I will remove them

from tending the flock so that the shepherds can no longer feed themselves. I will rescue my flock from their mouths, and it will no longer be food for them. (34:7–10 NIV)

The lambs are in danger of being destroyed by those we call shepherds. Shepherds become a threat when they feed off those under their care. Both the Old and New Testaments are loud about such things. And many of us have seen the destruction of vulnerable lambs in churches and in Christian organizations. It is a gravely serious matter that deserves our response in both word and deed, not only for the sake of the vulnerable but also for the sake of our God. Complicity and silence only add to the damage; they do not extricate us from it.

A Case Study

A young man recently out of seminary was hired to serve as the youth director for a large church. It was a small youth group, but over the course of his first two years, it grew exponentially. He loved his work. However, he became uneasy about some things he witnessed. He noticed three women visiting the senior pastor with increasing frequency. He returned to the church office one night because he had forgotten something and realized the pastor was in his office with one of these women, and no one else was in the building. He approached the pastor about his concern regarding the appearance of such a meeting. The pastor reassured him that nothing untoward was going on, saying, "Don't you trust me? I have been senior pastor here for fifteen years. Surely you have more faith in me than to suggest such a thing."

A few months later, two girls told the youth pastor and his wife about being sexually abused. One girl said her abuser was a church elder. The abuse occurred when she used to go to his house to play with his daughter. The second girl said she was raped by one of the young men in the college ministry. Both girls were fourteen. The youth pastor considered himself a mandated reporter. Out of courtesy, he went to the senior pastor to let him know what he had heard and to tell him he was reporting the abuse. The senior pastor was angry and told him not to call anyone. He said, "I am the God-ordained authority in this church. You must respect that and follow my decisions. I will handle this. I know this elder [they played golf together weekly] and am certain the accusation has no basis. I will also speak with the accused college student. He is a good friend of my son." The youth pastor left very troubled. He and his wife decided that he should report the abuse, even though he had been told not to. The girls were alleging that a crime had been committed.

Upon learning of the report, the senior pastor, filled with rage, went to his elder board and presented a twisted, untrue scenario, and the youth pastor was fired for insubordination, for an inability to submit to the church's order of authority, and because he was deemed full of pride. He was told to leave immediately. He was not allowed to speak to the youth. He was given no severance. The youth were told that the elders had to let him go because he would not submit to the church's authority, which they felt was setting a bad example for the youth.

Though many may not recognize this, the church spiritually abused everyone in the congregation. The name of God, the Word of God, and the authority of God were used to silence accusations and attempts to expose darkness. The congregation was deceived and confused. The people were told how to think and feel and what to say. The elders followed a sinful shepherd like blind sheep and used the power tools of deception, intimidation, condemnation, manipulation, and isolation to manage and effectively erase the crises. Those in power did

135

all they could to silence the truth. They presented the problem as something other than abuse. The youth pastor "disobeyed" those God had put over him. The victims were exaggerating. They misunderstood. The courageous youth pastor paid a high price for speaking truth and trying to protect the vulnerable. He is also likely to get a stinging review when he applies for another position. The two girls were ignored. They were discarded in the house of God. The damage to their lives and their faith was overwhelming. That damage was inflicted in a place that should have been a refuge for them.

Voices were silenced. Power was abused in order to accomplish that. The human voice is silenced by anything that is dehumanizing. It is dehumanizing to abuse, to cover up, or to outright lie about abuse. To treat any human, a person created in God's image, as less than human is destructive to their personhood, their identity. The God who is called the Word intends for those created in his image to have a voice. God places value on the interior/personal voice. He created us to speak. He does not want that voice silenced or crushed.

The Power of the Exterior Voice

There is another powerful voice besides the interior voice, one that has profoundly shaped all of us. The interior voice of each individual is heard against the backdrop of an exterior voice, which is often loud and strong. It may be that of another individual, a family, a church, a culture, an institution, or a nation. In the church, the exterior voice is church leadership—which claims to represent the voice of God.

As we have seen, we often unthinkingly assume the righteousness of the context in which we live. We fail to listen carefully to what the exterior voice does and does not say, and we fail to take the measure of both in the light of God's Word.

Almost by osmosis, we absorb and obey the external voice of our context, even when it is speaking falsehood about the reality of abuse. Leaders speaking on behalf of that exterior voice, for example, may say that people who expose abuse are bad (self-serving, attention-seeking, misguided, etc.) and need to be silenced because they threaten the good work the system is attempting to do in God's name. Even when the exterior voice is silent, it continues to communicate loud and clear. Church leaders may speak about protecting the church or may double down on claiming to have the authority of God, yet their silence in the face of abuse tells another story. So we have a deadly combination: silence paired with the voice that speaks falsehoods that seem true.

This process goes one step further. The silence about wrongdoing is rationalized and affirmed as a desire to protect the name of our God. Such rhetoric from leadership fosters interior silence in the victims and in the followers. In the example above, the victims spoke. The youth pastor spoke. Both did so in an attempt to bring truth and light. If voices are not heard or are ignored, they often fall silent, either under duress or due to hopelessness. The silence of leadership and the denial of the abuse further silences victims, mutilates faith, and destroys hope.

Victims assume that God is also silent. Many people have asked me through the years whether they can find help for restoring their sense of safety in the house of God. That such a question must be asked is frankly damnable.

The Startling Contrast of the Good Shepherd

The One we follow called himself the Good Shepherd. In the Old Testament, *shepherd* was a title designating the highest servants of the Lord, servants who, like our Lord, bent lowest to care for the flock. Of the Lord it is said, "He shall feed his flock like a shepherd: he shall gather the lambs with his arm, carry them in his bosom, and shall gently lead those that are with young" (Isa. 40:11 KJV). Contrast that description with the story of Kenny Stubblefield in chapter 5.

Jesus said that thieves and robbers preceded him (John 10:1). But he goes on to say, "I am the good shepherd. I know my sheep and my sheep know me. I provide security and food for all. I lay down my life for them" (vv. 14–15). Note the contrast. His primary goal was protecting the sheep. The goal of the thieves and robbers was to protect self and system. The only lives laid down in our case study were the lives of the victims, the youth pastor, and the members of the congregation. The shepherds got away unscathed. This same Jesus told those who followed him, "Feed my lambs. Tend my sheep" (21:17). Paul later used this same analogy when he wrote to the leaders of the church in Ephesus. He said, "Take heed to yourselves, and to all the flock, to feed the church of the Lord, which he purchased with his blood" (Acts 20:28). If the roots of the church are not producing shepherds who follow these instructions, then something is significantly corrupted. The name of our God is profaned.

Any church leader who feeds themselves rather than feeding the sheep is a counterfeit shepherd. Anyone in a position of power within the body of Christ who abuses a lamb or hides the abuse done to one the Good Shepherd knows and calls by name has profaned the name of our God. God stands against them just as he did the shepherds in Ezekiel 34. Should not his church stand with him against such shepherds? Yet if we say anything, we say, "It was just a mistake. The leader is under a lot of stress. Aren't we supposed to forgive and forget?" God's people have continued supporting corrupt shepherds and have failed to deliver the flock from danger. We have passed abusive wolves along to other flocks without telling the truth that they're receiving an enemy of the sheep and of our God. God says to cease! Leaders have failed to look like the Good Shepherd. So have his people when they have followed along behind those who are not obedient to God's call regarding wolves dressed as sheep. In so doing, they have followed shepherds off a cliff. How is it that lambs are abused in the house of God and then tossed aside because they disturbed the order of things?

God says further on in Ezekiel 34 that he himself will seek those lost and driven away by his so-called shepherds and will bring them back. He will bind up the broken and strengthen the sick (vv. 11–16). We look nothing like him when instead we bind up the abusers and strengthen their position. We seem to have forgotten our Lord's words recorded in Matthew 7:15–16: "Beware of false prophets, who come to you in sheep's clothing but inwardly are ravenous wolves. You will recognize them by their fruits" (ESV). They look like sheep, but they are insatiable, greedy, and voracious wolves. If they look like sheep, how can we know? We know by the fruit of their characters—the fleshing out of their identity. When someone tells us that a person we know has sexually or physically abused them, we think, *I know that person; it cannot be true.* Scripture says that our hearts are utterly deceitful; we don't even know our own hearts. We have a hard time believing that. Scripture says that Jesus trusted no one because he knew what was in all people (John 2:24). We say, "I know that person; I trust them." But Jesus says, "I know them; I do not trust them; I know what they are capable of." He would say that about me, about you. Scripture tells us that God does not judge by appearances but according to righteousness. We judge by what we see and hear, and we assume we know the heart.

Jesus said that the tares grow alongside the wheat. There is a mingling of the counterfeit and the real. The tares look so much like the wheat at first that we cannot tell the difference.

But no matter how closely together they are planted or how alike they seem, in time the difference becomes clear. We can see that the essential power of those who name the name of Christ has been imitated by false power. True purity has been counterfeited by false sanctity. We can know, sing, repeat, and teach the Word of God, yet its true harvest may be absent in our lives, our homes, and our world. We must never assume that someone who is gifted verbally and has theological knowledge is spiritually mature. Sometimes that leader is a narcissist, working the system and the people in it to feed themselves.[5]

Discernment of character becomes possible only in manifestation. Paul says that the life of Jesus is to be manifest, made plain in our mortal flesh, unmistakable and undeniable (2 Cor. 4:10–11). We are known by our fruit, not just our words. We are known by what comes out of us. The final test is in our character, for it is the fruit that tells us about the inner life of the tree. Henry Burton said, "Conduct is character in motion; for [humans] do what they themselves are."[6] Think about our case study. What characteristics were manifest, made flesh in undeniable ways, in the leaders? Despite their words, the arrogance, lying, demeaning, and silencing were evident. If we know the Word of God well, we can hear words as twisted, self-serving distortions of what God truly said.

What Does the True Church Look Like?

Wherever in the middle of suffering and sorrow the Son of Man plants a child of his own, obedient to the King, there he is working toward the healing of the wound, the drying of the tear, and the turning of weeping into an anthem of praise. There he is establishing his kingdom. God influences the world through his people, not through organizations. We, not a building or organization, are his body in this world. Our effect depends on the extent to which the Word we know has altered our lives. The natural development of Christ in us is humility, righteousness, and service. These are the marks of those in whom God is incarnate. The marks of true Christianity are always those of likeness to Christ. Unnatural development results in loftiness, pride, and dominance. As Jesus said, test yourself and others by this: the person who is greatest, let them be a servant. True ministry is not domination won in the name of Christ or the claiming of power to rule over others for our own sakes. Whenever the church seeks dominion or loftiness or expresses itself in pride, it becomes the refuge of unclean things.

Matthew 21 describes Jesus's triumphal entry, culminating in his entrance into the temple, where men were trafficking unclean things in the name of God. Jesus drove the traffickers out by making a big mess and a loud racket. He called them robbers who had profaned God's temple, making it a safe workplace for those who despoil their fellow humans. According to Jesus, that den had to be destroyed for the sake of the people who were being despoiled. Religious observance becomes blasphemy under such conditions, an opiate that dulls and deadens the spiritual sense when it ought to be transforming character into Christlikeness. When such evil is happening in the house of God, it ought to be ended, for the sake of victims certainly but also for those who are deceiving themselves.

It is fascinating to see what followed Jesus's actions. After the traffickers in unrighteousness were driven out, the blind and the lame came in, and Jesus healed them. Children came in shouting, "Hosanna!" which means "Save now!" Its Hebrew root means "to help," "to aid," or "to succor."[7] All those who needed assistance—the vulnerable, the lame, the blind, and little children—came *after* the temple was cleansed of robbers, those who fed on others. Before, God's temple was profaned. Now it was graced and honored and a bit like a hospital and a nursery.[8] The chief priests got angry and asked if Jesus could hear what was being said. They evidently heard the voices of the little ones as disruptive and needing to be silenced. Sound familiar?

Jesus responds with Psalm 8:2:

> Through the praise of children and infants [the most
>   vulnerable]
>   you [God] have established [strength] against your
>   enemies,
>   to silence the foe and the avenger. (NIV)

Great things are accomplished through the little ones, the weak ones, the vulnerable ones. When those cries for seeking, saving, protecting, and refuge are heard and honored, *then* our enemy is silenced. What power the voices of the little ones have if we heed their cries! When we silence the cries of the vulnerable ones (child or adult), we are not protecting God's house. In fact, we are desecrating it, amplifying the voice of the enemy in the house of our God. When we follow our Lord, we bring his redemptive power to bear, not only in the lives of victims but also in our own. God takes the sins against the vulnerable and uses their cries to call us to transformation into his likeness. I know, for he has used the battered, broken lives of many victims to do his redemptive work in me. They have been his gift to me.

Jesus drove out those who took what was not theirs, those who made his temple unholy. He then welcomed the little ones and the weak ones, those who establish strength against God's enemies and silence his foe. How then can we, the people of God, silence the little ones and the weak ones when they speak out and say, "Save us now"? We thwart God's redemptive work in his people and in this world when we protect our institutions and titles and positions rather than the vulnerable.

May the body of Christ be bold in driving out unrighteousness and welcoming the vulnerable ones, thereby establishing power against God's enemies and silencing his foes. May we go with love and truth into the dens of robbers, no matter where we find them, be they in our pews and communities or in our pulpits, and transform them into places filled with the glory of our great God, who became vulnerable for us.

ten

Christendom Seduced by Power

All of us as Christians have one foot in secular, mainstream culture and the other foot in Christendom, our Christian culture. Many of us in the older generations are at least a bit frightened by secular culture's direction and influence on younger generations. We all long to be comfortable somewhere, to fit in, to feel at ease, at home. We allow ourselves to think of Christendom as a safe place, so we may be less discerning than we are with secular culture. We do not like to feel uncertain, awkward, or vulnerable. We breathe in a familiar culture of the Christian world, unaware of its toxins.

I fear many of us have confused Christendom, or our little corner of it, with Christ. They are not the same. They have never been the same. Institutions, organizations, ministries, and systems are not Jesus Christ. They are simply systems and places created by humans where God's people gather to worship, learn, and serve. Nor is Christendom even the same as the living body of Christ. Jesus himself told us that there are tares among the wheat, wolves among the sheep, and white-washed humans who only look like believers, sometimes even in leadership.

This is an admittedly complicated issue, but we need to recognize that Christendom is a system, both merged with the culture that surrounds it and trying to sustain itself separately. And Christendom, like all institutions under threat, uses resources, energy, and power to protect itself. If you doubt that, watch what happens when a case of child sexual abuse by a pastor is exposed. Speaking truth is often considered a threat to the church, a mind-boggling reaction when God makes it very clear that the true church is to bring light into darkness. That means seeing things as they are and calling them by their right name. Christendom has used Scripture to sanction slavery, racism, domestic violence, sexual abuse, and other cruelties our God hates. Some corners of Christendom today have, I fear, become less interested in truth and more interested in power. We have acquired fame, money, status, reputation, and little kingdoms. Yet at the same time, we are steeped in pornography, marriages are failing in large numbers, abuse is covered up, the next generation is turning away, and we tolerate leaders in our organizations and pulpits who feed off their sheep. As we've already observed, there have been many recent headlines about Christian leaders and Christian systems that look nothing like our Lord. Christendom is not Christ. We must not be deceived.

Christendom as a System

You may recall from chapter 6 that a system is a combination of parts forming a complex unitary whole and working together toward a goal. As we saw in chapter 9, systems designed by God for the purpose of blessing his people can stand together, use God's name, and simultaneously destroy human beings.

Systemic abuse by a group or organization that carries God's name is damaging beyond words. Many victims I have known have spoken about the crushing they experienced in such systems. Having been abused by someone in the system, they ran to the shepherds. Those shepherds ignored, silenced, rejected, and blamed them. The abuse of the "Christian" system multiplies exponentially the damage done by a single perpetrator.

Think back to your childhood. Recall playing outside, falling, and skinning your knee. What was the first thing you did? You ran to a parent for comfort, help, and healing. What happens when there is no refuge because the parent is using drugs or full of rage or blames the child's "stupidity"? That child lives in the reality that no one will enter or care for their pain. On top of the wounding, the child experiences rejection, a judgment of worth, and a loss of hope. The multiplied pain is life shaping. The lessons taught are lies: you are not worth my time; it is your fault; you are interfering with more important things. Whether done by a parent or a church leader, such rejection of an injured child teaches hideous lies about God that get burned into the soul: he does not see; he does not care; he blames you for what happened. Those lessons are not easily discarded. They settle in and saturate a life. Sadly, victims, adults as well as children, often do not distinguish between Christendom and Christ. What has been enfleshed is a gross misrepresentation of Christ, but many do not know that is the case, and their faith and hope are crushed.

The Seduction of Christendom

All of us long for meaning, purpose, connection, and blessing. The systems of Christendom offer us these things. In our hungering, we often fail to assess the systems or their leaders, who promise the fulfillment of our longings. Hitler promised to fulfill the longings of the German people for bread and dignity. He promised to restore morality. Much of the German church followed him. Just as there is a gravitational force in the physical world, there seems to be one in the spiritual realm. The spiritual words of an earthly kingdom lure us through our own longings. We whirl like satellites in that system's orbit, believing in the promised gifts and blessings. We are easily blinded to the fact that the force of gravitation is coming from humans and their words, not necessarily from God. We grant our love and obedience to earthly kingdoms rather than to God's kingdom. When spiritual words are used, we are often led to believe those kingdoms are identical. They are not.

Leaders and followers alike can be deceived. The primary deception that seems foundational to many is the strong belief that the kingdom of our God is an external one, here and now, measured by human standards. It was a deception Jesus's disciples believed (and longed for). Power, large numbers, fame, and global acclaim are presumed to equal God's blessings. Our longings attach to the promises of leaders, and we submit ourselves blindly to the promised "kingdom" of success. Breathing in the culture of Christendom without examination, we baptize it, support it, and pledge loyalty to it. Our support often requires overlooking lies, abuse of power, sexual abuse, greed, deception, haughtiness, and compromise with earthly powers. As is often true in the secular culture, we simply accept what happens without discrimination or examination in the light of the Word of our God. We forget that external kingdoms of all kinds have failed perpetually throughout human history and will continue to do so. Our continued longing for an external kingdom leaves us vulnerable to seduction.

There are seductions inherent in serving God. They are subtle dangers; many don't see them and are seduced away from their first love. The work of service is often seductive, luring us away from love and obedience to the Master. Many times someone starts out believing they are called by God and instilled with a God-given vision. Somewhere down the road, when the vision has grown, the demands are great, and the pressure is on, the servant becomes obedient to the work and its demands rather than to Christ. Decisions are made based on what will succeed, bring in money, or promote growth. "The work must not be allowed to die," they tell themselves. It is God's, after all. So the life of Christ in the leader begins to die. The worker then is no longer a servant of the Master but a servant of the work. It is a good work. It may be a work into which God called them. It may have borne fruit. But the worker is now focused on the success of the ministry rather than on standing true to Jesus Christ.

Oswald Chambers said, "Beware of anything that competes with loyalty to Jesus Christ. The greatest competitor of devotion to Jesus is service for him."[1] When God's work seems to call us to neglect marriage and home, solitude and study, we have traded masters. When character is secondary to accomplishments, we have traded masters. When the demands of serving shape our character into something other than a reflection of the character of Christ, we have traded masters. The master called "service" will drive us unrelentingly until we drop. The master of service is not concerned about our character, does not care whether we are the incarnation of what we teach, and does not care whether we delight the heart of the Father. It cares only that the work succeeds. The master of ministry is never satisfied. Big must get bigger and truth must be evaded at all costs, if exposure to that truth might damage the external kingdom. This seduction occurs in both leaders and followers. Any threat to the system leads followers to circle the wagons and protect the leader and their position, the system, and the pretense of truth. Take heed lest you be seduced.

Another seduction works like this: As we get involved in caring for others, caught up in the drama of their lives, keenly aware of their pressing needs, we can easily be seduced into forgetting that we are first a sheep before we are a shepherd. If we forget that we are a sheep, we will become focused on getting others to move, change, and grow while failing to seek out our Shepherd and the green pastures and still waters he has for us.

If we care for God's sheep long enough, we will have plenty of experiences that will enlighten us as to why God calls his people sheep. We will watch people do stupid things, follow other sheep into ravines, move away from the flock, and get devoured. We may catch ourselves muttering about "just a bunch of stupid sheep," and we will get frustrated, angry, and proud, as if somehow *we* are the shepherd over all these stupid sheep.

Have you been called to shepherd the lambs of God in some fashion? You may shepherd as a pastor, a teacher, a counselor, or a parent. Do not forget that long before God called you to shepherd, he called you first and foremost to be his lamb—a silly, stupid lamb who does stupid things, follows others into ravines, and allows themselves to get devoured. You are a lamb who must stay very close to the Great Shepherd. That is the best and wisest way to lead other lambs. They will follow you there. Your value as a shepherd depends on your life as a lamb, a weak, foolish lamb utterly dependent on the Shepherd. How will you know anything about shepherding if you do not stay close to the Great Shepherd?

When the work of shepherding leads us to pride, judgment, superiority, or deception, we have forgotten that we are a lamb. A shepherd who is not first a lamb is a dangerous shepherd and has ceased to follow the Good Shepherd. Our primary identity in life, if we are to be of eternal value to the Father, is not that of a shepherd but that of a lamb. Take heed lest you be seduced.

The third seduction is when the work crowds out our relationship with God. "The measure of the worth of our public activity for God is the private communion we have with him."[2] Our yardstick is success; God measures by the private relationship we have with him. Our personal relationship with God is what renders us fit for ministry. Is a relationship with Christ a thread woven richly into the tapestry of your life, or have you become so taken up with Christian work that you have no time for the Christ whose work it is?

Christian work will compete with our relationship with God. What irony! But we must expect it to do so. The very work God calls us to do becomes that which distracts and seduces us away from time with him. But we will acquire what is needed for the work of God in our hidden, worshiping life as a Christian. Do you want to be prepared, equipped, fortressed, and protected? Then cultivate a relationship with God.

In working with those serving God in many arenas, I have found that many do not pray. I've heard leaders say, "I'm not much of a prayer person" or "I have not really learned how to pray." In other words, I can lead a church or organization, make it grow, teach, and preach without prayer. Prayer can be seen as something done in public services or at meals but frankly rather impractical and evidently not necessary. The work demands to be done, the programs need to be run, and the people need to be tended. Who has time for prayer? Yet the Lord we profess to serve considers prayer a central part of the work rather than simply preparation for the work. Prayer is the path toward fruit-producing, fruit-abiding work. How foolish we are to think that we can carry out the work of God without continually talking to him and listening to him.

Do not presume to do the work of God from any foundation other than an ongoing relationship with him. How can we possibly think we will have wisdom, untiring love, and strength to persevere unless we sit daily at the feet of the Savior? He said, "One thing is needful" (Luke 10:42 KJV). Only one thing is needful. Only one thing is necessary. Not two, not several. Getting the work done is not that one thing. This was Martha's lesson. Her work was needed. She was tending to Jesus and his disciples. Her work mattered, but it was not "the one thing." Worshiping, learning, listening at the feet of the Master is the one thing, always. Take heed lest you be seduced.

There is a fourth seduction. Instead of first and foremost loving and obeying Jesus Christ, we are often lured into following human leaders. We like being part of something successful. We long to be with the "in crowd" of Christian leaders, if not as another leader, then at least as a follower. We are doing ministry right. We are part of something special. We have the correct doctrine regarding such and such. It is very easy to follow an earthly leader or a system rather than Christ. Pause and consider some of the well-known leaders of recent years who have destroyed ministries, others, and themselves. We seem inclined to follow whoever glitters rather than carefully discerning their character. Many blind guides have led sheep into the pit in this way.

In Psalm 20:7, David said this:

> Some trust in chariots, and some in horses;
> but we will remember the name of the LORD our God.
> (NKJV)

Do not trust in a successful leader, ministry, or growing numbers. Do not trust in fame or accolades. Do not trust in books sold or great knowledge acquired. Those things are not Jesus Christ. He did none of those things. Leaders, do not measure yourselves by such standards but by the character of our Lord. Followers, do not follow any leader with all the above trappings who bears little or no likeness to Christ. There is only one Lord, and he is neither a human leader nor a human system.

Examining Longings

As leaders and followers, we have longings. They matter. Are we thirsty for love or hungry for safety or significance? Do we long for respect, accomplishments, and honor? There is nothing wrong with such longings. They are human. But they also make us vulnerable to powerful individuals and systems that promise to fulfill them. They can lure us into thinking we are the one who can ride in and do something newer, bigger, and better. They can also lead us to see in a leader what we desperately long for, leading us to fail to discern a wolf in sheep's clothing. Sadly, sometimes the systems of Christendom promise to fill us up, those unassessed promises are believed, and great damage is done.

There are leaders and followers who long to be famous, the best, the biggest, the most effective. Those desires are presented as being for the good of the members of the system. We have the key to evangelism. We are going to reach the world for Christ as never before. We will solve the orphan crisis in this country. We will reach the unchurched. But what happens when something threatens that human system and the toppling of its dream? What is the response to an exposure of sexual abuse or a report of domestic abuse in a leader's home? What is the response to an accusation of fraud or a misuse of funds? In those places, who gets protected? What is most protected by the system? The leaders? The power structures? The existence of the institution? How does the faith proclaimed by the system respond? What fruit does it bear?

We must assess the systems and the leaders with whom we connect. We must assess character, theirs and ours. No system and no leader can satisfy the human soul. The well from which we drink should not be a captivating preacher or a certain kind of worship experience. There is nothing wrong with those things, but they are not Christ.

The Character of Christendom

Here are some important things we need to remember about systems and leaders in Christendom. First, nothing and no one can represent God accurately except by a likeness to Jesus Christ. We have learned that leaders whose teaching benefited us were unfaithful, rude, and demeaning to workers behind the scenes. Often because of outcomes and growth, such behaviors are excused and hidden. Faith that pleases the heart of the Father reveals itself not in external measures such as growth and numbers but in character and Christlikeness. One who follows Christ bears the fruit of the Spirit in every nook and cranny of their lives. The faith of a true Christ follower emanates in kindness, gentleness, self-control, patience, and faithfulness. These describe the character of a follower of Jesus, one who is living out of grateful love to Jesus Christ. Anyone who does not manifest this fruit, no matter their accomplishments and great success, is not following Jesus. They are not growing in likeness to Christ.

Second, Jesus did the will of his Father no matter the cost. He did not work to preserve a system, even one originally ordained by God. He worked to expose and transform the human heart and destroyed external systems to that end, even those dedicated to him. He did this with the temple whenever it began to exist for its own purposes. He did so for the sake of individuals, both leaders and followers. If we, with him, want to be a part of the kingdom that will someday rule all kingdoms, then we should submit to obedience to him and him alone, even if it costs us our systems.

Third, Jesus tells us that his kingdom is not external. It is not of this world. His kingdom exists in the hearts of men and women who love and obey him. Those people who bear his fruit in their character are where he resides. George MacDonald said, "How many are there . . . who seem capable of anything for the sake of the Church or Christianity, except the one thing

154

its Lord cares about—that they should do what he tells them! . . . . They leave him to vaunt their Church."[3]

Let's say you are a parent of a beautiful child who is full of life. Your child becomes sick, and the doctor tells you it is cancer. It must be treated, or the child will die. Treatment begins, and you watch your child waste away, listless, thin, and weak, the light gone from her eyes. You feel like you're losing her. All you want is her health returned and to see her running across the yard, laughing, once again full of life and joy. The treatment that appears to be destroying your child is the only road to health. You love her enough to put her through that treatment, though it breaks your heart to do so.

That is the heart of our Father when his people are full of cancer. Many refuse treatment to protect the external appearance of health, ignoring the fact that over time death will win. Our God is a consuming fire. That fire is love, a love that will go to any lengths to destroy the cancer. He longs for his body to bear his likeness more than he longs to preserve any external kingdom, even one that bears his name.

Remember the story of the fig tree? Jesus was returning to Jerusalem and was hungry. He saw a fig tree covered in luxuriant green leaves, the external appearance of a healthy tree. He walked over to see if he could find a fig but found nothing. Fig trees would normally produce fruit before the leaves, which didn't appear until summer, still some time away. The tree communicated a false message by its display of leaves. Our Lord used the deceiving, unfruitful tree as an object lesson. His people were not bearing the fruit his Father had called them to bear. Jesus condemned the tree to look like what it already was—sterile and barren—not because it had no fruit but because its premature display of leaves left the impression that it was a fruit-bearing tree. It was like a wolf in sheep's clothing.

The story is ultimately about the temple system that God had designed and ordained. The system was displaying itself as good and faithful to God, all the while not producing fruit. The previous day Jesus had left the city and, looking down over the temple, had wept. The temple goers had clothed themselves in luxuriant rituals and incense and proclaimed, as they did in Jeremiah's day, "The temple of the LORD!" They had forgotten that their hearts were the temple God longed for, just as he does today. They had forgotten that love of God and others was the sacrifice that pleased his heart. He longs for the fruit of righteousness to be born in his people. He is not interested in luxuriant greenery that gives the external appearance of growth.

Sadly, Christendom has often mimicked the world or conflated itself with the powers that be. We have worked toward building an external kingdom. Throughout the ages, Christendom has joined with—gotten in bed with—secular powers such as the state and the king. When that happens, the people of God lose their prophetic voice. Instead of bringing light to human affairs, the church blends in so well that it can hardly be seen. Light illuminates; it does not conceal. By investing in Christendom rather than in Christ, we have dimmed that light and lost our way.

We who are to expose and root out corruption have been corrupt. Where is the light that illumines? Where is the salt that purifies? And where, oh where, is the repentance in Christendom for calling itself the body of Christ when it has so often utterly failed to follow its Head? A body that does not follow its head is a very sick body. That is as true in the spiritual realm as it is in the physical realm. And our Head, in his love for humanity, broke down every barrier, including the barriers of race, gender, class, ethnicity, religion, and morality. He welcomed and loved us all and called us to himself so that we might become like him. We would all be excluded if he had not.

I'm sure you remember the story of the great crowd of people in dire need. They had followed Jesus and were hungry, all five thousand of them. He fed them and had twelve baskets left over. I think we might call that successful service. The people certainly did. They proclaimed Jesus a prophet and wanted to make him king. They wanted an immediate, external kingdom. The crowd wanted something that God wants: Jesus as King. How easy at such a juncture to let the externals dictate. The people seemed ready. They desired what God had ultimately established as his goal. Jesus will be established as King over all. He will sit on the throne, and the nations will bow down. He will rule the hearts of humans and all the externals.

Jesus then did a very strange thing. His response was to withdraw to a mountain by himself. It appeared that he lost his opportunity. It looked like everything was set up for him to accomplish what he had come to accomplish, yet he walked away. Why? Because he served his Master; he obeyed his Father rather than the people and their longings or demands. His choices were not dictated by opportunity, by the promise of success, by need, by the desire of the people, or even by the goodness of the goal.

When the day comes and people push you toward a goal you believe is good, remember Jesus. The work is not your master; he is. The goal must be his goal, achieved in his way. The timing must be his. And you must be wholly his. Do not be owned by the goals of service but by the Master alone.

Leaders, followers, and systems can all easily deceive us, whether they are secular or part of Christendom. But people and systems are both known by their fruit. Many have been deceived by trees that appeared full of the promise of life and were not. Hold close the truth that good fruit is *always* produced by those who bear the likeness of Christ. That fruit is the *character fruit* of his Spirit in our lives. It is not found in our gifts, though they are certainly given by God. Paul says that we can speak with an angel's tongue, understand theological mysteries, and give money to the poor and yet not look like our Lord in character. Oration, knowledge, brilliance, and philanthropy are not fruit born of the Spirit in our lives. Do not become a counterfeit or be duped by one. Follow hard after Christ, not after Christendom, with its allure and promises. Christendom is not Jesus Christ. Seek for him to be the culture in which you live and move and have your being.

PART 3

Power
Redeemed

eleven

Redemptive Power
and the Person of Christ

The Lord we follow, God incarnate, had to navigate secular and religious cultures of his day when he came to earth as a human person. He was so despised that both the Roman Empire and the Jewish nation, who hated each other vehemently, joined forces, colluding to kill him because he would not bow to their rule. Miroslav Volf has said, "The single most significant factor in determining whether a religion will be implicated in violence is its identification with a political project and its entanglement with those trying to realize and protect that project."[1] The temple leadership did exactly that with the Roman Empire.

Jesus says, "I do nothing of my own initiative [self as center], but I speak the things the Father taught me. And he who sent me is with me. . . . I *always* do those things that are pleasing to him" (John 8:28–29). Because Jesus never wavered from choosing love and obedience to the Father as the driving force in his life, he was a threat to both individuals and systems of his day, a holy dissident with a disruptive presence and disruptive words.

His character threatened Rome's powerful ways—warfare, conquering, bloodshed, and oppression. It also threatened the religious system, which exercised power and fostered rigidity, empty ritual, exclusion, and judgment. He who was the foundation of that system looked nothing like it. He opposed all that was contrary to the purposes and character of the Father in individual, social, national, ethnic, and religious life. He sat apart from those who stood together, and in doing so, his faithfulness to the Father led to his extermination . . . or so they thought.

What can we learn from Jesus as we traverse our own treacherous territory? We often think of such obedience as *costing* us. But when something other than obedience to God is our master, we are starving ourselves spiritually. The star of Jesus's way, the food for his soul, is God and God alone. It is not a doctrinal center. It is not a racial, tribal, or national center. It is not a set of moral rules. If we are to understand Jesus's mind, his heart, and his choices, we must know his Father, not the systems. Christ is explainable not in terms of a culture but only by knowing the Father. This Christ disturbs massive systems and turns the world upside down. We, as his people, are to be like him.

The Character of Christ in Human Hearts

First, we need to reiterate that Christ is building his kingdom in the hearts of men and women, not in the externals we have come to love, protect, and praise. The temple in Jerusalem was a beautiful structure, filled with God-ordained rituals, leaders of great knowledge and doctrine, and thousands of worshipers. Beautiful structures, a performance that moves hearts, theological brilliance and correctness, and large audiences are things Christendom praises and prizes today. But the purpose of God in all those endeavors down through the centuries was first that his people should worship *him*, because he alone is holy. People are made fit to worship him because of the Lamb that was slain.

Second, God's people were to flood the earth with truth, love, humility, food for the hungry, honesty in business, welcome to the strangers, and care for the disenfranchised as an outgrowth of their worship. God gave his people power to bless the world. Instead, they were manifesting judgment, division, oppression, corruption, and disregard, all while they were slaying lambs and making money from it. God's people were so far from understanding who God was that when he showed up in the flesh, they did not even recognize him. The external trappings meant nothing to God. Such externals are not proof of his presence, let alone his approval, even when they have their origin in him.

Jesus says that what comes out of us, from our center, defiles us (Matt. 15:11). Do we understand this? It's not the political atmosphere in our country that defiles us; it is not the rampant immorality in this world that defiles us; it is not the pressure of expectations for excellent grades, more money, more fame, or many followers that defiles us. If such external things produced defilement, then Jesus himself would have been corrupted. He came here, to this death camp, and remained full of the life of God. He remained pure because nothing unclean was *in him*. What did not exist in him could not come out of him. We cannot bear apples if we are a maple tree. And that failure is not in the soil, rain, sun, or gardener, though all those things matter. The failure to produce apples resides in the nature of the tree.

Think about a situation in which a Christian leader has been exposed for sexual immorality. What happens first? Usually lies are told. "I did not do it. I just went in to help the sex workers, and I ended up caught in a sting." This response is a misrepresentation, a twisted telling of things, a camouflage—such responses often use spiritual language. When that no longer works, what happens next? "Well, yes, I did it but . . . I was depressed, my marriage is a mess, I was so pressured by ministry." In other words, "What was happening outside of me defiled me. My immorality did not come from within." But if we look carefully, we can see that what came out of the person when faced with exposure was deception of self and others and attempts to convince us they are actually fine, good, and righteous. They were simply sideswiped by external things. The external circumstances may indeed have been difficult, even excruciating, but somewhere in the heart was a hook, a lie, a coddled desire so that in the context of those circumstances, the hidden corruption of the heart was exposed. Or as Oswald Chambers says, "Crisis reveals character."[2]

Jesus says, "Hear and understand. It is *not* what is outside of you that damages you. It is what proceeds out of you. Nothing can come out that is not in" (see Mark 7:15). We know this is true in the physical world. "A cup brim full of sweet water cannot spill even one drop of bitter water however suddenly jolted."[3] The jolt exposes what is in my cup; it does not create the contents. Hence, by their fruits we shall know them; we shall see who they really are by what grows from within. We know the contents of a heart by what comes out of it, not what is around it. No one is ruined in a crisis whose soul has not already been weakened by choices made in day-to-day life. We do not wake up one day immoral. Immorality is practiced quietly and in small ways over time. We are anesthetized by the opiate of self-deceit—until the cup is bumped and we are exposed.

If we are truly like the person of Christ in the kingdoms of our hearts, then what flows out of us will resemble him. Where it does not, we need to ask him to do whatever is needed *in us* for change to occur. People will know our source of life by the outflowing waters they taste.

Jesus Is Light

"God is Light, and in him is no darkness at all. If we say we know him and yet walk in darkness, we lie and do not practice the truth" (1 John 1:5–6). Light penetrates, searches, invades every nook and cranny. Light brings health and growth to all living creatures, plants and animals alike. The entrance of light anywhere exposes reality. Light brings truth. It's often not visible itself, but it illuminates all else. It's also not changed by what it reveals. Light shines on dead animals, sewers, and rottenness, exposing yet remaining unspoiled. That is our God. That is why Jesus was uncorrupted by corruption. That is why he was uncompromising with compromise.

The person of Christ *is* Light. In him is no darkness at all—none, not even a spot. No matter how much he encounters darkness, is surrounded by darkness, or exposes darkness, he remains light. He is not contaminated by what he touches. He touched us and remained pure. He does not traffic with the darkness of earth or hell and does not, even with intimate contact, ever become dark. "The Light shines in the darkness, and the darkness did not overpower it" (John 1:5). The power of Christ is his embodiment of light. He sheds light wherever he goes, in both word and deed. How do you suppose Rome or the religious leaders felt about that light? They wanted to turn it off. And how do you suppose Mary Magdalene, the Samaritan woman, or Zacchaeus felt about that light? They rejoiced in it. Jesus's light was either opposed or welcomed; its presence revealed the heart of the one on whom it was shining.

We, God's children, *say* we have a relationship with this God who is Light. Then we should welcome his light. He says, "If you say you know me and yet walk in darkness, you are a liar" (1 John 1:6). That is crystal clear. We cannot deal in darkness while claiming a relationship with light. If we say we walk in fellowship with God, who is Light, and pursue pornography, or cover up another's repeated sin, or grasp at power or fame or self-righteousness, we lie. If we say we walk in God's light and speak harshly to a spouse, crush a vulnerable soul, demean another online, or arrogantly treat others as inferior, we lie. If we do indeed walk with him, such things will be exposed for what they truly are, not weaknesses, not responses to pressure, not a bad day, not a heavy schedule, not means to a good goal. Such things are nothing but high-handed rebellion against a holy God.

Darkness conceals and disguises. It distorts, hides, and disturbs vision so that things appear other than they really are. Darkness varnishes over blemishes. We use the darkness to hide ourselves from ourselves, from others, and from God. We hide behind harsh speech, calling it righteousness. We darken our hearts with excuses, justifications, and lies. In practicing darkness while professing light, we sin. And sin leads to death. It is not simply physical death but also death of clear vision, death of righteousness, death of conviction. Often the things that enable long-term sin to continue are so much a part of the fabric of our lives that we don't even see them anymore. That is why Jesus called the Pharisees blind guides.

"In [Jesus] was life, and that life was the light of all mankind" (John 1:4 NIV). Let's shine light on two statistics: 64 percent of Christian men and 15 percent of Christian women view pornography at least once a month.[4] If we *say* we have fellowship with him and walk in darkness, we lie and do not *do* truth. We are deceiving ourselves, and the light is not in us. We write and talk and some of us scream about issues such as homosexuality and abortion, but we hide some of our own choices and do not do truth. We absorb degrading, humiliating, violating pictures of others who were knit together by God in their mother's wombs and created in his image. Do we really think we can feed on such a diet and then treat others with dignity and respect? Do we believe we can absorb darkness and give off light? The mind is being trained in the ways of darkness, and we continually deaden ourselves to truth in order to maintain that darkness and feel OK. Many have said to me, "They are just pictures." For the record, I have worked with those who ended up in those "just pictures," forced into participating in pornography and trafficked online. I have seen girls as young as eight years old, living on the streets and being prostituted, trafficked, and picked up for pornography films. And we, who call ourselves God's children, are funding that world by our participation in it.

Understand also that statistics from various sources show that we in the evangelical world are both divorcing and battering our spouses as regularly as our secular neighbors are.[5] And we *say* marriage is sacred. We are to love. How? In the same manner as Jesus loves us. Yet research shows that we Christians are also the most likely to object to living next door to someone of another race.[6] Our words are harsh, judgmental, and even cruel toward those who are unlike us in some way, even fellow believers. And God says there is neither Jew nor Greek, barbarian nor Scythian, slave nor free (Gal. 3:28). God is Light, and in him is no darkness at all.

We've all heard many grievous stories about Christian leaders and their immorality, their financial fraud, and their arrogant, demeaning, and abusive leadership. We have often protected those in high places who have given us glimpses of the darkness in their lives. Why? Because they have a phenomenal following; they are brilliant and articulate; they have amazing gifts of music, or speaking, or . . . you fill in the blank. And so rather than bringing light, we join them in their darkness, excusing and justifying and compromising and leaving those who have been victimized unheard and uncared for. Do we not see that we are willingly, in the name of ministry, leaving these leaders, not to mention their victims, in the dark? Talk about blind guides! In protecting them, we are complicit, folded up with their darkness. The most righteous action one can take toward some people is bringing the facts of their lives into the light. It is righteous to expose an abuser. It is unrighteous to cover their crooked deeds. It is righteous to expose a leader's arrogance. It is unrighteous to minimize or excuse it.

Charles Spurgeon said, "Leniency to the dishonest is cruelty to those whom they injure."[7] Dietrich Bonhoeffer said, "Nothing can be more cruel than the tenderness that consigns another to his sin. Nothing can be more compassionate than the severe rebuke that calls a brother back from the path of sin."[8] Is that not what the God who is Light did and does for us? "Look at who you are," he says, "and come to me."

Jesus Is Love

God is love. "The one who does not love does not know God" (1 John 4:8 NASB). Love is not created but flows from God himself. He sees the truth of humanity's rottenness and decay, yet he pursues us in love. That is an amazing statement. When we see rottenness and decay, we want either to distance ourselves or to flee into deception. In essence, like the priest and the Levite in the story of the good Samaritan, we walk on the other side of the road. Love sees by the light what is true and yet enters in. And we know from Paul's beautiful words that this love is patient beyond measure, kind to the unkind. Such love is "not arrogant or rude, and it doesn't seek its own benefit. It is a love that rejoices in truth," in the light that exposes (1 Cor. 13:4–6). Love is shown in a word, a touch, a meal, a cup of cold water, an apology, an affirmation, a story read to a child, or any of a hundred such things that have the capacity to bring the love of God to this world and delight his heart. God's love is a love that moves toward a person; it does not wait for them to approach.

His love in us goes forward to others, as they are precious to him even if they are not precious to us.

We are told, "If a person says, 'I love God,' yet hates their brother, they are a liar" (1 John 4:20). God wants command of our hearts' love, to reign first in our affections; he wants to be our center. The testing ground of the truth of that reign is our love for others. Is God your center? Then out of you will flow love . . . even to the unlovely. God first loved us; we love him, and the evidence of that wholehearted love of God is love of others. Our love for God should expend itself on others. If it does not, we are liars in proclaiming that we love God. We have deceived ourselves.

Christ is God's Love incarnate, stooping to the uttermost depth to eradicate the poison, the deadly virus that will lead to the genocide of the human race if it's not stopped. He who is our Head is the Lamb slain. There is no depth to which we can go where he will not search us out, whether we are victim or abuser or both. He is not pursuing us, however, so that we feel better. He is pursuing us in love in order to bring light, and he longs for us to stand with him against the darkness and the infrastructures of our own lives that evil has erected so that we can pursue others with his love, for his name's sake.

Walk in the Light of Love

Pause and consider the hidden infrastructures of your life. If you know Christ, then there is within you a Loving Indweller. He walks through the rooms of your heart; he knows your points of view. He listens to your words and thoughts. He traverses the back alleys of your life where others do not see. He longs for every gate and avenue and closet to be always open. He who walks there is the sworn enemy of evil and darkness. He longs not to be barred or hindered by doors you have locked against him. He wants to fill the whole place with himself, with his righteousness and infinite love. He wants to travel your soul, bestowing benedictions. Out of that certain knowledge and your soul's submission to his light and love, he wants you to go out into the world and walk as Christ walked. He is the incarnation of Psalm 15:

> O LORD, who shall sojourn in your tent?
>   Who shall dwell on your holy hill?
> He who walks blamelessly and does what is right
>   and speaks truth in his heart;
> who does not slander with his tongue
>   and does no evil to his neighbor,
>   nor takes up a reproach against his friend;
> in whose eyes a vile person is despised,
>   but who honors those who fear the LORD;
> who swears to his own hurt and does not change;
> who does not put out his money at interest
>   and does not take a bribe against the innocent.
> He who does these things shall never be moved. (ESV)

Lest you feel too small for the pursuit, remember that Jesus also walked as one who abides in God. Walking is not extraordinary. One foot in front of the other. It doesn't glitter and awe. It is commonplace. It can be boring, repetitive. But walking as Jesus walked transforms the ordinary. Abiding means walking with the heart and mind of Christ. Are you learned? Do you value the mind? That's a good thing. But whose mind is preeminent in your life? Yours? A particular theologian's? A respected scholar's? Or the mind of Jesus Christ, that mind set on things above, things not material? Is your mind set on conformity to the mind of God, with no higher allegiance than obedience to the Father? Do you long for a mind like Paul's—a mind not governed by those things we humans value, such as nationality, tribe, blood, knowledge, tradition, school of doctrine, morality, religion, or our own opinions? Do you have a heart that is always leaning toward the heart of the Father? Is your passion increasingly knowing and obeying the heart of the Father?

The power of a person is found in likeness to Jesus Christ. It is not found in brilliance, gifting, knowledge, position, verbal power, reputation, or fame. It is found when a mere person, such as yourself, flings open the corridors and closets of their life so that they are full of the light and love of God. That person, full of living water, will alter any landscape in which they walk. That person will help fill the earth with God's glory.

For this eternal outcome, our High Priest entered this genocidal world, this death camp. He became like us so that we might be like him. The kingdom of Hitler is no more—nor is that of Caesar or Stalin or Mao Tse-tung. Over the years and generations, we have also seen many kingdoms in Christendom rise and fall, some quite recently. Our world continues to see new leaders who rise and then fall. "The whole world lies in the power of the evil one" (1 John 5:19 NASB). But that's not the end, is it? The verse that follows says that we also know that the Son of God has come. He manifested the heart of the Father in everything he did and said. He did not rise and fall. He fell and then rose. He is here now, by his Spirit, with you and me. I pray we listen for him and let him search our hearts and our lives so that we might walk as Jesus walked.

May we not follow the siren of culture, institution, or family, even if someone baptizes the system for us. May we not be seduced by the allure of Christendom nor heed the spoken Word of God when it is used to sanction something utterly unlike him. We must be shrewd as serpents, astute, sharp-eyed, wise, and vigilant. We must know Christ so well that we can discern what is unlike him no matter the seductive or religious garb it wears. But in our shrewdness, we must not be toxic or poisonous. We must be harmless. We are to bless the nations, not become one. We are to bring salt and light and grace and bread. We must starve anything else but Christ in our lives. We must go among those we live, work, study, and worship with and restore dignity to image bearers who have been labeled something else. We must walk with those who bear burdens, walking with humility, not with arrogance. We must fall first in worship at the feet of Christ and fall second as his servants in his world. Ultimately, we must live as those who do not fit in, for we ourselves don't fit in—neither in culture nor in Christendom. We are citizens of heaven, not of earth and its kingdoms (even those we have erected in his name). We are servants of the Most High God alone. We are in fact the undocumented immigrants of this planet—aliens and strangers. We are citizens of another country, but while we're here, we serve, often behind the scenes, those citizens we meet, no matter their category. We are called to serve faithfully on behalf of the Lord who placed us here.

Dietrich Bonhoeffer, a man who stood for Christ and against not just Hitler but also the Christendom of his day, penned this benediction from prison: "May God in his mercy lead us through these times; but above all, may he lead us to himself."[9]

twelve

Healing Power
and the Body of Christ

Jesus uses his power to protect, to expose, and to restore dignity. He calls his people to be in the world using our power under his authority, displaying his character by speaking truth, shedding light, and tending and protecting the vulnerable. How does this become a reality in the lives of individual Christ followers?

There was once a man who held a powerful position and infamously used his power corruptly for his own gain. He didn't have much physical power, for he was small. He did have a cunning mind. He lived in an evil city, full of tax collectors and priests. He was a chief tax collector and a rogue, getting rich at the expense of the poor by extorting more than Rome demanded. How do you suppose people felt when this rogue showed up? Glad or fearful? Threatened or safe? Honored or demeaned?

One day a noisy crowd gathered in the streets. The man was curious to see who was getting so much attention, but he was too short to see over the crowd. So he climbed a tree to see what the fuss was about. When Jesus arrived under the tree where Zacchaeus was perched, he looked up and said, "Hurry, because today I must stay at your house" (Luke 19:5). Zacchaeus came down and welcomed Jesus into his home. The Lord of the universe bent down to small, self-serving power, corruption, and greed in order to accept the hospitality of a rogue. He went into the home of Zacchaeus, and the doors closed. We have no record of what happened inside. In receiving Zacchaeus's care, Jesus was clearly tending to him. He used his power to bestow dignity. That's not how power usually approaches those lower down the ladder. Jesus came to serve, but he entered into the lives of those whom others disdained, by allowing himself to be served.

Eventually, the doors open, and we see Zacchaeus has changed. He takes a stand and says publicly, "Look, Lord! Here and now I give half of my possessions to the poor, and if I have cheated anybody out of anything, I will pay back four times the amount" (Luke 19:8 NIV). Zacchaeus now used his power for two things: to give and to restore. He went into his house mastered by greed. He came out mastered by truth and compassion. He went from power abused to power demonstrated in humility, from greed to graciousness, from self-serving to giving. The story ends with Jesus interpreting the incident for us. The Son of Man came to seek and to save that which was lost: the little, the trapped, the blind, the lost, the corrupt, the user, the rogue (v. 10). His power turned an abuser into a giver and a restorer *just like himself*. That is what *all* power does when harnessed by the Lord Christ.

In the Name of Jesus

My father was an Air Force colonel. No matter where we lived and no matter what job he was doing, he lived and moved and had his being under that name. He was a man of his uniform all the way through. His carriage, his manners, his speech, his words, his actions, how he governed his time, how he spoke to those over or under him, in uniform or out, on the base or off the base, always demonstrated integrity. That's who he was. He taught us the importance of reflecting that as well.

My brother and I were the colonel's kids, and so we, along with our father, represented the government of the United States. And we were expected to act accordingly. We learned how to greet officers who came to the house. We said, "Yes sir" and "Yes ma'am." We learned to stop our play and stand at attention when the flag was lowered no matter where we were on the base. My father served in the name of the United States. Since we went with him, we too represented that name.

Today, I represent a different name. I represent the name of Jesus. Living with and before others in the name of Jesus is a far more massive and serious task than representing the United States at the age of six or ten. I'm now far more aware of the enormity of such a calling. How would God have us think about our hearts, our power, and the kingdom of our God?

Power and Authority

Jesus manifested all power by coming in the flesh to this earth, living with us in a way that explains the Father. He manifested his eternal power by wearing our skin, entering our world, traversing through our small minds and hard hearts. What he did was stunning—it looks nothing like how we use power. And now, as his children, we are called by him to live our lives in a way that helps others understand him more clearly. Everything about our humanity is to be brought under his authority.

When we select leaders in the church, we look for brilliance, charisma, and knowledge, all forms of human power. The apostle Paul says no. He describes his own authority as not according to the flesh. His power didn't come from human personality, human brilliance, or any human gift or activity. Was he brilliant? Yes. Was he gifted? Yes. But he laid those qualities aside if they hindered his care for another soul. He claimed to take captive every thought, perception, or purpose and make it obedient to Christ.

We must yield completely to the governance and power of our God. Our characters should be shaped by him. We are not to simply "appear" to be like him in word and deed. Often such things are merely a front. Our hearts and minds, where others cannot see, must be actively under his rule as well. The discipline of living under the governance of God in the hidden places is a lifelong work. It begins with humility, by being on the ground before him and never getting up. We are his creatures, created in his likeness for the purpose of service to him first, then flowing out to others.

How are we to think about power and authority in our own lives? How has it shaped us, and how do we exercise it? How are we to use power in the name of Jesus to bring healing? The power of choice is inherent to being human, and it has eternal consequences. "Choose for yourselves this day, this minute, whom you will serve," says Joshua (Josh. 24:15). In the Gospel of Matthew, we see Jesus's deep agony over the refusal of Jerusalem to follow him: "I wanted to gather your children together . . . , *but you were not willing*" (23:37 NKJV).

C. S. Lewis wrote about choice in a truthful, chilling way: "Every time you make a choice you are turning the central part of you, the part that chooses, into something a little different than it was before. And taking your life as a whole, with all your innumerable choices, all your life long you are slowly turning this central thing into a heavenly creature or a hellish creature. . . . Each of us at each moment is progressing to the one state or the other."[1] Our small, everyday choices make an eternal difference.

Jesus used power not to rule but to influence, to invite, to welcome, and to transform. Will we use our God-given power of choice to seek certain outcomes or to live under the governance of God and rely on him to accomplish his purpose? When we are in Christ, no nationality, no government, no race, no gender, no status, and no prejudice rules our choices and actions. To be in his image in this world is to live and look like the One we call Lord. To call him Lord is to give him the ultimate authority. That authority is his eternally, but he gives us the choice to bow or not. If we choose to follow him, we bow to one authority and only one: his. Our treasured and protected local distinctions, divisions, and preferences fall away as we find our home and our unity in what is unseen and in the humility of Christ.

The Power of Humility

Philippians 2:3 gives us a remarkable picture of humility: "Do nothing from selfishness or empty conceit, but with humility of mind regard one another *as more important than yourselves*" (NASB). Living utterly under the governance of God in accordance with this Scripture would have turned slavery on its head. Indigenous peoples would have been blessed, not crushed. Jim Crow laws would never have existed. If we lived this way today, our thoughts regarding poor and rich would be transformed. Marriages that are crushing, silencing, or abusive would not exist. Workplaces that cheat and oppress and overwork would be transformed. Christians who live under the governance of God and God alone would live and work in transformative, redemptive ways that are utterly unlike the world and its powers.

There is more. Paul goes on to say, "Do not merely look out for your own personal interests, but also for the interests of others" (Phil. 2:4 NASB). Laws and policies are generally formed by those in power. Organizations and systems are generally led by those in power. They are often governed by their own interests. Those we consider less than are often excluded. The bottom line financially is often the top-line concern. We divide, we segregate, we ignore, we silence, and we turn away those who do not fit into our human categories of nation, race, gender, financial status, and education. God says we are to actively consider others' interests anytime we do something. We are to use our power to care for their interests as well.

Why? Because the One we follow did not use his equality with God to his own advantage. He emptied himself, poured it all out and became like us so as to serve us. In doing so, he endured unimaginable suffering, humiliation, rage, dismissal, and an excruciating death. He used his great power in the service of love. If we do not follow Christ in these ways, we are in great danger. We will lose our way and fail to display the character of Christ. We should be humble because we are but creatures of the dust. We should have humility because we are sinners, blinded by deceptions we do not see. We should be humble because we belong to Christ, who led the way in humility and calls us to be like him.

Humility is the mark of Christ. It is the way of power used rightly. It is Godlike to serve in humility. He who sits on the throne was the servant of all while here, and on the throne he continues to serve us by his Spirit. We must know him well and deeply if his work is to be accomplished.

The Power of Love

To use our power rightly in this world, we must exercise it through love, as Christ does. To do this, we must first love the Lord our God with all our being. To love God is to be his, to reflect his character, to be governed by him, no matter the cost. To love God is also to love our neighbor—anyone made in the image of God. When we separate love of God and love of neighbor, as we often do, we are not loving God, for our God loves all humanity. By not loving someone in your life, you are not loving God. If we call Jesus Lord, then we are to do as he says. And he says that we are to love the Lord our God with everything we have, more than we love position, relationship, association, power, status, or fame. It is a high and narrow calling.

I have been struck recently by the fact that within Christendom we seem bent on prioritizing authority over love. Yet this is not how God deals with us. George MacDonald says, "Now what is deepest in God? His power? No, for power could not make him what we mean when we say *God*. . . . But let us understand very plainly, that a being whose essence was only power would be such a negation of the divine that no righteous worship could be offered him. His service must be fear, and fear only. . . . In one word, God is Love. Love is the deepest depth, the essence of his nature, at the root of all his being."[2]

Yes, pastors and elders have authority over the sheep. Husbands and wives have power over each other. But in Scripture, the primary characterization of these relationships is love. We seem to ground authority in position or gender and then require obedience to that authority. But *all* authority is Christ's, and any derivative of that power given to us is to be submitted to him *in love*. Our obedience belongs to him and him alone.

Any authority that is not exercised through love is a false authority. Paul says we are to follow after love, giving it the highest value. Love is the most excellent way, greater than all the other gifts we seek. To speak or teach without love is to do nothing but make noise. Love is the power of speech. Love surpasses prophecy, knowledge, and deep understanding of mysteries. And love surpasses those things that give the appearance of love but are not rooted and grounded in love. Such actions, Paul says, are nothing; they are deemed worthless. Love is to be both our motive and our power. It is important to remember these things so we can evaluate whether we are truly loving those we say we love and whether others who claim to love us are in fact loving us truly. We are often so hungry for love that we swallow the words of another without observing their character, which is unwise and unsafe.

What does the power of love look like? Paul describes it as patient and kind. It shares its abundance with others. It does not envy. It is not jealous of the ear when it is an eye. It rejoices in the acuity of the ear and is blessed by it. Love does not boast and is not proud. It does not elevate itself or puff itself up. It is not rude or impolite. It does not seek things for itself—notice, praise, or elevation. It does not seek silence or cover up for itself either. Love is not easily irritated or angered. In relationships, it does not keep score. It rejoices in truth. It speaks truth about the cancers of the soul. It bears all things. Love is the power that endures.

We who are Christ followers are to follow hard after love. We humans are easily deceived. We originally ran after fruit that looked good! Now we run toward the fruit of numbers, money, expansion, oration, and status. Our original purpose was like-ness to God. Our purpose today is the same: to be Christlike. Our purpose is not church growth. When growth—or any-thing else—is our aim, we will bow to whatever we must do to acquire that goal. God in Christ is our goal. And our God tells us he is Love. We comfort ourselves with our deceptions, using them like a blanket we wrap around ourselves, measur-ing things our Father does not measure: how many people are coming, how we are growing, how much talent we have. Our power in this world is not in those external things. We have no kingdom here. We do not even own ourselves. We are children of the Most High God, who became a hunted and migrating baby on our behalf. Jesus, knowing he had come from God, took a towel. If an earthly kingdom was the goal, then Jesus is an utter failure.

Jesus's master ambition was to please the Father. The test of our likeness to him is whether we use the power of love to descend, to enter in. Do you love God? Then go be a neighbor. Go enter into a life unlike yours and be the incarnation of the One who loves you eternally. The result will be true transformation. The love of God, first in Christ and now in us, is the most powerful weapon there is. When we walk in love with others, the response will be, "Now I understand the love of God, the graciousness of God, the steadfastness of God, because I have seen glimpses of it in you."

In the 1800s, Amy Carmichael went to India and spent the rest of her life serving the girls sold for temple prostitution in the Hindu temples. She opened her heart to the trafficked, the defenseless, and the enslaved. One day when she was speaking with some women about Jesus and his great love for the girls who were in bondage, a woman replied, "If this be so, you are as an angel from heaven to us. But if it is so, we want to see it lived. . . . *Can you show it to us?*"[3] That same question sits before each of us who names the name of Christ. If it is true that God himself came in the flesh to the brokenhearted, the small, the afflicted, and the vulnerable, that truth needs to be lived out so that the world knows it is real.

The Lady Ecclesia

One of the authors I've come to love is George Matheson, a nineteenth-century Scottish pastor and songwriter. Matheson describes the church, the bride of Christ, as the Lady Ecclesia.[4] We are the Lady Ecclesia. Christ paid a high price for us and loves us very much. He yearns for our hearts to match his and for our deeds to reflect his image. He longs to have us serve in this world as his representatives, as his like-minded servants to humanity, carrying his fragrance out into the world.

Our Master has called his Lady Ecclesia to follow him and to go out into the world he loves, into the dark habitations of cruelty where evil and suffering seem to reign. She has not always followed her Bridegroom. Sometimes she is fearful; sometimes she is greedy and self-protective. At times she has preferred comfort and familiarity to venturing out among the ground zeros of this world and those in her midst. But when the Lady Ecclesia was still quite young, a hundred years old or so, she went boldly into places where many feared to go, representing her Lord and refusing to accept cultural norms.

Baby girls were considered a liability in the first century AD. Female infanticide was not uncommon, and demographics in certain parts of the world were stunningly imbalanced male to female. Infant girls, often considered deformed, were killed by exposure. The law permitted them to be left outside the city on the dung heap to die; they were considered worthless.[5] But a growing group of people seemed to consider that judgment of the value of females an error. They went outside the city to the dung heap to find and rescue the abandoned baby girls. The decision was both risky and sacrificial. It required standing against the mainstream culture. It meant the giving of life, time, and goods to someone else's discarded baby girl, extending the circle of one's responsibility. It meant being devalued and disdained for stooping so low as to treat that which was deemed worthless as precious instead. It meant living sacrificially for the least of these. Who were these people? They were the bride of Jesus Christ, his Lady Ecclesia. She followed the Lamb who had gone outside the city gates to make the ultimate sacrifice, giving his life as a ransom for many who were deemed worthless. By his death, he judged them precious. His Lady followed him.

The call answered by Christ's first-century Lady is not unlike the call that confronts us in the twenty-first-century church. The question remains whether we will follow the Lamb both inside and outside the city gates as she did then. Will we pursue and rescue those seen as worthless in the eyes of this world and sacrificially work among them because they are precious in his sight?

Not so long ago, we began to learn about the garbage heaps of the Catholic Church that continue to be exposed. We now know of thousands of boys and girls, men and women who were thrown away to "protect" the church. We've followed the news of the boys thrown out by the Boy Scouts. We've read the headlines about the large number of victims of Larry Nassar and Jeffrey Epstein, one protected by position, the other by wealth. And now we know about the many vulnerable ones tossed aside as garbage by the Willow Creek Association, the Southern Baptist Convention, Harvest Bible Church, and the Sankey Orphanage in the Philippines. If we're honest, we also know that the discarded pile of victims is still rising and that many are still working feverishly to cover it up. There are untold stories yet to be heard. Any time we have tossed aside those who have been abused, we have committed "great whoredom by forsaking the LORD" (Hosea 1:2 ESV).

My father's life was rich with lessons, some coming from his experience of a disabling illness that eventually landed him in a nursing home, where he spent his last years. As his disease progressed, he lost control of his body. This athlete could no longer tie his own shoes, get up out of a chair, or walk down a hallway. My father had been a very capable man; he knew how to bait a hook, slam a tennis ball, ride a horse, tie his shoes, and walk. But he could not get his body to do what his head knew how to do. His body would not follow his head. I learned that a body that does not follow its head is a sick body. Jesus Christ is the Head of the church. Our Head has called us to follow him. Where we do not, we are very sick.

If you and I follow our Head, we will bring the character of God into flesh and blood. We will go where he went, looking

183

like him. We will follow him and be bent, shaped, and conformed to his image.

The Lady Ecclesia is to be conformed to Christ in all things. Sadly, we are often conformed to many other things. Rather than being part of a body that follows its Head, we tend to function as a body that follows familiar, comfortable, unexamined patterns. Sometimes we follow the rest of the church body in its sicknesses and deceptions. As my father's disease progressed, it shaped my father's body; it conformed his body into a contortion of its original self. Not following our Head always leads to deformity.

Listen to the voice of the God who is our Head speaking to the Lady Ecclesia down through the centuries:

> Lady, learn to do good;
> seek justice,
>   reprove the ruthless;
> O Lady, defend the orphan,
>   plead for the widow. (Isa. 1:17)

I recently tweeted this quotation from my book *Suffering and the Heart of God*: "Christianity does not look like praying and singing and giving money while ignoring the screams, unspeakable suffering, filth and death of others. Christianity is not about calling others 'them,' somehow unlike us, not human, and deserving of their suffering."[6] One of the replies to that tweet grieved me deeply. It read, "Really? Because it sure looks like that from the outside." The response to my tweet suggests that its author has seen anything but love from the church. Christendom's failure to use its power to bless demonstrates a great lack of love. This injures our Lord, who said that what we do not do for the least, we do not do for him. What a sad contrast to what John said: "By this will all people know you are mastered by me, if you love one another" (John 13:35).

Aristides of Athens said this in the second century of the new church when he appeared before Emperor Hadrian: "Behold! How they love one another."[7]

Christ, our Head, is the embodiment of love. He did not recoil from the lowliest human. Isaiah describes him in this way:

> The Spirit of the LORD is upon me,
>   because the LORD has anointed me
> to bring good news to the afflicted.
>   He has sent me to bind up the brokenhearted,
> to proclaim liberty to the captives
>   and freedom to the oppressed
> . . . .
>   to comfort all who mourn. (61:1–3)

The highest and most holy entered into our world through the lowest door.

One of the most precious scenes in the New Testament is in Luke 24, when two disciples walked with the risen Christ, not recognizing him until he "was known by them in the breaking of the bread" (v. 35 ESV). Having just accomplished the most stunning event in time and eternity, Jesus was known not by his glory, power, entourage, trappings, or number of followers but by his nail-scarred hands breaking bread. *That* is our God. When the body of Christ fails to look like him in these ways, she is sick. She is not following her Head—no matter what labels she has used, assurances she has given, or certainties she has proclaimed.

The Function of the Body

Though manifested in varied ways, the ultimate function of the body of Christ throughout time is to fulfill her sacred calling to live in ongoing fellowship with her Head, Jesus Christ, and be under his governance in all things. The people of God who compose the body of Christ on earth are to live fully and faithfully under the lordship, authority, and mastery of Jesus Christ. If we are to be mastered, we must know him. We cannot follow the thoughts, longings, ideas, or plans of another unless we know them deeply. And we do not know them deeply simply by someone else telling us about them. We must pursue such intimate knowledge on our own, over time and through concerted effort by listening, working to understand, learning how to think as they do. We will neither know them nor represent them well unless we do these things. We must not passively rely on leaders or teachers to tell us about our Head. We must seek him, listen to him, follow him. We will fail to do as he asks, and we will not be able to discern a corrupt leader unless we know Christ well.

When we look at the church scene today, sadly, we see divisions. Not long ago in the United States, we divided the church into black and white and in doing so defied our Head, who welcomes all. We will never know how much we have lost as a result. We are divided by suburb and inner city. We are divided racially: black, white, Hispanic, Asian, and Indigenous. We are often divided by politics, wealth, education, or a particular issue. But our Lord says that *all* parts are necessary.

The body of our Lord consists of many members. Each member's primary relationship is with the Head, and relationships between members flow out of that connection. Every member of the body of our Lord is important, no matter their status in life, their abilities, their position, their race or gender, their wealth or education. No one can say to another, "I do not need you." The foot cannot say to the hand, "I do not need you." And most amazingly of all, the *head* cannot say to the foot, "I do not need you." The highest cannot say to the lowest, "I do not need you." All parts (including you), cooperating and living under the mastery of our Head, are necessary. When we assign greater and lesser as categories in the body, we are no longer under the mastery of our Head. When we let divisions and differences divide us, then something other than our Lord Christ is ascendant. When we turn aside from those wounded in our midst, according to Jesus, we have turned aside from him. If anyone is left out, we don't look like the body that will ultimately stand before his throne.

Suffering and God's Heart

The book of Hosea is a picture of the heartbreak of God. The sins of God's people had wounded his heart. His people had gone after other gods; his bride, his Lady, was pursuing another. Idolatry is a religious counterfeit. It often looks very real; otherwise, we wouldn't be deceived by it. In his excellent book on Hosea, G. Campbell Morgan says that idolatry is religion seeking to worship God falsely represented.[8] The Israelites' worship of Moloch was exactly that. Israel was deceived by its false ideas of God. We are deluded into thinking that if something looks like God, sounds like God, has the goal of pleasing or being like God, it must be good. Such deceptions always distort humanity and always break God's heart.

I have learned during my decades as a psychologist that you can tell what is most important to someone by what they protect most vociferously. A person using drugs will protect access to the substance on which they're dependent. If caught, they may cry and apologize and promise to stop, but internally they are already searching for ways to pursue what they want more than anything else. Looking at Christendom today, I frequently see that when the church is threatened, its energy goes into protecting the system. We love and worship the system or our church more than we love and worship Jesus Christ. That is why we engage in complicity, in cover-ups, in silencing, in

187

name-calling, and in threats. If those don't work, then bit by bit we offer up some half-truths, testing to see what is acceptable and what will stop the exposure. The goal is to protect the institution, not to stand in the light.

As I have listened to the stories of many victims, I have learned that there are countless loves dearer to us than love for God. Jesus's poignant question "Do you love me?" comes to mind. Loving anything more than we love him amounts to idolatry, and that may be the root of the problem. I don't mean putting carved figures up and worshiping them. No, it's far more subtle and deceptive. Think back to the Hebrews, God's chosen people, called to bless the world, rescued from slavery, and having received God's thoughts by way of his servant Moses. They knew God. He visited them and taught them how to worship him alone. Yet somehow his people—people like us—judged it good and right to create and worship a golden calf! We are his people, those he has visited and taught how to worship him. Have we not made golden calves out of statistics, money, fame, position, and our external systems?

Look instead at the One "greater than Solomon" (Luke 11:31). His statistics are measly, his wealth nonexistent. He had no home, and the temple of his Father was being desecrated and trashed by corrupt religious leaders who hated him. The strongest sign of God in him was his ability to continually bend his will to God's to the extent that he had the power to lay down his life. He has called us to do the same. He asks us to use our God-given power of choice to follow him in *his* ways, not our preferred ones. He has called us to follow him, even if it means our temples collapse.

Hope in the Valley of Trouble

These are troubling times. The church of Jesus Christ finds itself in a Valley of Achor (*achor* is a Hebrew word meaning *trouble* or *affliction*). We learn of this Valley of Trouble in Joshua 7, where the unfaithfulness of one man, who took for himself that which belonged to God, brought trouble and death to that valley. Yet God promised he would "make the Valley of [Trouble] a door of hope" (Hosea 2:15 NIV).

Some of you reading this have been beaten down and crushed by the misuse of power in the church. You have experienced sexual abuse, spiritual abuse, name-calling, and dismissal because you did not do what you were told. Some of you have done the crushing. You have believed that protecting an institution is a godly choice. You may have lied or hidden the truth to that end. You have convinced yourself that the work is too important and too big to let "a little thing like that" destroy it. In doing so, you have enabled cancer to grow in the body of Christ. Others have been quietly complicit, believing that God prefers to preserve our "good" institutions with their good goals. Perhaps we are not troubled enough by these times.

Remember that Jesus was crucified in part by a system ordained by God for his worship and the blessing of his people. Consider his arraignment: conducted in the wee hours of the morning, which was against civil law; conducted in the house of the high priest rather than in the temple, which was against religious law. Leaders broke laws in order to kill Jesus. Many of our systems have followed this same path.

Let's be honest. To our shame, we have often treated people the way Jesus was treated. We have humiliated, lied, crushed, blamed, and degraded. We have done so to those of other races. We have done so to victims of many kinds of abuse who disrupted our order and called us to enter in. We have worked in secret. We have not dragged such things to the light. We have acted illegally and refused to report child abuse. We have not acknowledged that domestic abuse and rape are against the law. We have covered up our deeds and our verdicts to protect our ways and our systems. In doing so, we have followed the

Sanhedrin rather than Jesus. We have acted not as blundering disciples but as those who were flagrantly disobedient. And Jesus has to heal the wounds we have caused. This is a hard place, but it is good that many are beginning to see and are deeply troubled.

I have said repeatedly that the voices of victims today, of those abused and violated and crushed in our "Christian" circles, are in fact the voice of our God to his people. Through those we have mistreated, he is turning on his light, exposing us to ourselves (and others), pointing out the cancer, and calling us to fidelity to him alone. In essence, this is what Jesus said when he declared, "Let the little ones come, for my kingdom belongs to such people as these" (Matt. 19:14). They are a prophetic voice to the church. They are canaries in the coal mines of Christendom. Victims are vulnerable, struggling, wounded, broken, and in need of extensive care. They are a picture of who we all are before God. And we are to be a picture for them of who he is with us, the One who came from the heights to the depths for those who were vulnerable, struggling, wounded, broken, and in need of extensive care.

This Valley of Trouble is God ordained, and in this place, he is calling his people back to himself. In John 12:27, Jesus says, "Now is my soul troubled; and what shall I say? Father, save me from this hour: but for this cause came I unto this hour" (KJV). It was through the troubling of Jesus Christ that the door of hope was opened for us. It was the troubling of God, the sorrow of God, his broken heart that opened the door of hope. The cost to him in opening that door shows us the severity of sin. When we love the work more than the Master, we are contributing to that cost. If we will listen and see and repent, then we will enter into the great troubling we have caused in the lives of vulnerable humans, seeking to live in his likeness, bringing joy to his heart rather than sorrow. We will do so though the foundations of our buildings shake and the mountains of our little kingdoms crumble into the sea. Ultimately, we will hear the chorus from Revelation 5:13:

> Then I heard every creature in heaven and on earth and under the earth and on the sea, and all that is in them, saying:
>
> > "To him who sits on the throne and to the Lamb
> > be praise and honor and glory and power,
> > for ever and ever!" (NIV)

Postlude

In conclusion, come with me to two countries—Cambodia and Bulgaria—where I learned some valuable lessons and clear, godly truths.

First, Phnom Penh, Cambodia, where I traveled to teach people from ten countries about trauma and abuse. While there, I was taken to see some of the genocide memorials. As you may recall, the Cambodian genocide was carried out by the Khmer Rouge in the 1970s under the leadership of Pol Pot, resulting in about three million deaths. The Khmer Rouge first forced people out of their homes, their jobs, and their cities. Then they took the fathers and executed them. They separated mothers and children. They separated siblings. People were put in labor camps and torture prisons. Do you hear the layers of devastating loss upon loss?

When we went to the Killing Fields in Cambodia, we saw a place of trees and water and mass graves, some still not excavated. Walking on the boardwalk, we passed large depressions in the earth where the dirt had settled when it rained. "Bones continually rise to the surface when it rains, as do pieces of tattered cloth," said my guide. The Killing Fields were a place of both beauty and horror. I sat down, stunned, almost unable to think. As in Rwanda and Auschwitz, I had no words . . . I who earn my living with my mouth. I recalled the words of Elie Wiesel: "How is it possible that men, women, and children were being burned and that the world kept silent?" And his father's reply? "The world? The world is not interested in us. Today, everything is possible, even the crematoria."[1]

The church has its own killing fields. They are made up of every abused, misused, oppressed human being down through the centuries that the church of Christ has ignored, silenced, or thrown out. Child sexual abuse, rape, domestic violence, verbal and emotional abuse, the twisted and crushing use of power, said to be derived from Christ but really used to feed the self or the system, all contribute to the killing fields. We can kill a soul by any of these means. It seems clear that God is calling us, as he did the Israelites, to see, to listen, and to stop believing deceptive words that somehow lead us to hide or silence abuse and call it protection of the church.

In the midst of the Cambodian Killing Fields is a tree, a massive and beautiful creation of our God meant to provide shelter and shade. It's called the Killing Tree, because it's where the executioners killed babies by slamming them into the tree. The tree is covered with memorial items such as bracelets and rings and notes. And why were the children killed in this place? For the sake of cleansing. "What is rotten," said Pol Pot, "must be removed." Such words hid ghastly deeds done in the name of purity, wholeness, and protection.

And oh, that Killing Tree. It is very old, the kind of tree you look at and wonder what stories it could tell. It reminded me of Treebeard the Ent, a giant, treelike creature and ally of the free people of Middle Earth in J. R. R. Tolkien's *Lord of the Rings* trilogy. But the Killing Tree was no ally. The sign says, "Killing Tree against which executioners beat children." Why? So they would not grow up and seek justice for their parents' deaths.

They were silenced so they would not threaten the system. Our Lord tells us he loves justice. God also watches as we silence, threaten, and toss aside the vulnerable ones in our circles. I asked God what he was thinking and feeling as he watched such atrocities.

Please understand that the damage was done not just to the victims. Horrific damage was also done to the killers. Hideous damage was done to the participants, the complicit parents, the priests, the soldiers, and the neighbors—human beings destroying their own souls, sometimes even for God's sake and in God's name. When we hide sin in God's church and permit abuse by those who call themselves God's servants, we are aligned with deception and ungodliness in the name of Jesus! Where is God in the midst of such evil? Why does he allow these things to happen? What is he feeling and thinking? These are questions that stories of abuse and terror have raised in me over the years. God has taught me something of his answer to such questions. His answer comes by way of another killing tree. It is an odd one, though. It is not a tree where the "other" was killed for the sake of cleansing and purity. It is a tree where the Most Pure, Most Clean was himself killed for the sake of the dirty, the filthy, and the evil ones. It is a place where those in power took purity and holiness and executed them. Our lives and our eternities are based on that tree, that killing tree we call the cross. There too it seemed as if God had left. He was silent; darkness covered everything; Jesus was alone, rejected, despised, cast out. Sounds like a victim, doesn't it? He who has all power blessed us and then bowed, allowing human power—power used to protect place and position and institution and tradition, power that rendered the temple a safe place for predators—to destroy him. But they had it wrong, didn't they?

The power of Rome in bed with religious leaders crushed and killed many people. The power of religious leaders continues to crush people today, some of them in our own churches.

The God-Man on that killing tree bore Auschwitz, Rwanda, and Cambodia. He bore our arrogance and self-protection and deceptions. He bore our willingness to sacrifice others while telling ourselves we are preserving his church for his name's sake. He bore the great suffering of those used and abused and silenced down through the ages. He has called us to follow him in these ways, to places where we find ourselves overcome with grief and loss, stunned by the magnitude and the cruelty, places of utter despair. I pray I never recover from the experiences I've had of such evil. But as I sat and pondered in Cambodia, I saw the parable.

You and I live in the killing fields. We live on a planet full of beauty and horror, which strains both heart and mind. But there is no one on this planet, no matter how brilliant, rich, strong, healthy, or anything else, who will not face grief and loss during their lifetime, eventually facing their own death. Such things are woven into the fabric of this world. We do not want to face it. We feel little and afraid. Our own fears easily lead us to abuse our power so that we feel bigger, stronger, sure we are on the right side and protecting our places—for God, of course. Where is hope or strength in such a place? Where is strength to follow the One on that tree who openly condemned the things that create killing fields? We want to cover ourselves with power and safety, even if it means the vulnerable are thrown out. We want to hide behind our education, training, theology, and positions so that the little ones do not expose or disturb us. Yet we are called, like our Lord, to bend down in love and say, "Do not hinder them. . . . Bring them forward, for *they* are what God's kingdom looks like" (Matt. 19:14).

In another country, Bulgaria, I taught counselors from several countries who are working faithfully in the killing fields we call *trafficking*. I visited the capital, Sofia, and learned the history of this beautiful country. My guide told me that when World War II began, Bulgaria proclaimed neutrality. In 1941, anti-Semitic legislation was forced on Bulgaria by Germany. The people protested. In 1943, they were commanded to deport all non-Bulgarian Jews to the Treblinka extermination camp in Poland, a literal killing field. Some in high positions pressured the government to cancel the deportation, and the czar did so. A third time the Nazis demanded, and the Jews were loaded on railroad cars headed for the concentration camps. Several powerful men—a military commander, a legislator, and others—stood on the tracks and said, "You can take them, but you must kill us first." The Germans released them. In this instance, Elie Wiesel's father was proven wrong when he said, "The world is not interested in us."[2] There were exceptions. Bulgaria is one of the few nations honored at Yad Vashem, the World Holocaust Remembrance Center in Israel, as Righteous among the Nations. In 2013, Bulgaria celebrated the seventieth anniversary of those refusals to bend to an evil power and the saving of almost fifty thousand people. They called it the Ceremony of the Ungiven. Shouldn't we consider victims and the vulnerable to be the "ungiven" of the body of our Lord?

In ancient Israel, the priests set apart six cities of refuge as sanctuaries, places of safety for those who had committed accidental manslaughter. They offered refuge for people who had actually killed someone. Shouldn't our churches be places of sanctuary for those who have been intentionally abused? How is it that children and adults are being abused in a place of sanctuary? And how is it that when we learn of such things, we hide them? Do we think our God does not see?

When you and I stand before God, we will stand *ungiven* because of the killing tree, the cross. Jesus said to his enemy, "You can take them, but you will have to kill me first." Are we not to do as he has done? How is it then that we protect abusers, who will inevitably abuse again? Given their habituated self-deceptions that lie deep within, it is highly likely. How is it that we throw aside the abused because they disturb our sanctuaries?

The ungiven are not to be those in power, our institutions, or our external kingdoms. The ungiven are to be those who are vulnerable and preyed upon. I'm afraid we frequently get this backward. We will not sacrifice those in leadership, those we think we know, and those who have power. *They* become our ungiven rather than the victims we freely dispose of "for the sake of God's work."

May you and I be those who see the killing fields and the souls that lay there, that *we* have put there. May we stand in the light of God's killing tree, knowing that by his blood we are blessed to be part of the ungiven. May we use our power to work to bring in and care for those who have been sent away to die. May we have the humility to acknowledge our wrong choices and decisions that have damaged precious souls. We have done damage by our actions as well as by our inaction and our ungodly silence. May we be those who go out to the fields looking for the lambs who have been wounded by the wolves dressed as sheep and like our Lord carry them to safety and a refuge from which they will *never* be given.

And finally, may we, in this our day of sin and darkness and failures and troubling among the people of our God, pray with Daniel, who also faced such things:

> O LORD, great and awesome God, who keeps his covenant and mercy with those who love him, and with those who keep his commandments, we have sinned. . . . We have done wickedly and rebelled, even departing from your precepts and judgments. . . . O LORD, righteousness belongs to you but to us shame of face . . . because we have sinned against you. . . . And now, O LORD our God, who brought your people out of the killing fields with a mighty hand . . . hear our prayer and cause your face to shine on your sanctuary, which is desolate. Incline your ear and hear; open your eyes and see our desolations, and the people who are called by your name. . . . O LORD, hear! O LORD, forgive! O LORD, listen and act. Do not delay for your

Postlude

own sake, my God, for your church and your people who are called by your name. (Dan. 9:3–19)

May we, the church, be known as those who, in likeness to our Lord, use the power he grants to expose evil and protect the vulnerable. May we celebrate with him, and in his name, the Ceremony of the Ungiven.

Acknowledgments

Every one of us is something that the other is not, and therefore knows something . . . which no one else knows: and . . . it is everyone's business, as one of the kingdom of light and inheritor in it all, to give his portion to the rest.

George MacDonald[1]

No book is the product of one person. This one has been woven together by many people—both around the globe and close to home. All have given their portion to me, and I now pass it on to you.

I am forever indebted to those who have suffered unspeakable things at the hands of twisted power. They have courageously been my teachers and honored me with their trust. I understand truth more clearly and love more deeply because of them.

This book began with Katelyn Beaty, acquisitions editor for Brazos Press. She brought both the idea and the challenge to me, and I am very grateful to her. I have benefited greatly from the Brazos team. Careful editing, creative marketing, and a commitment to this work have been demonstrated by all.

My office associates have walked with me faithfully. We have been in the trenches together, have witnessed the evil of power abused, and have shared a love for our Lord, who set power aside to draw us to himself. My colleagues Barbara Shaffer, Phil Monroe, Beverly Ingelse, and Carol King read early drafts and offered much wisdom. I also value the input of Sheila Staley and Kyle Howard, who provided insight into the perspective of African Americans.

My office manager, Bethany Tyson, and her assistant, Dara Becker, run an efficient, gracious, and ethical office. They have proven flexible and offered a smile when my schedule got in the way of theirs.

Evangeline Hsieh graciously provided invaluable research in tracking down and citing sources.

Karen Wilson is a dear friend, a "word woman," and a lover of Christ. She brought the gifts God has given her and poured them into this work. Both this book and its author are better for her presence.

My husband, Ron, as always during these projects, kept both of our lives running smoothly. His faithful presence in all areas of my life has been unwavering.

Finally, all glory to the Lamb who sits on the throne and holds all power. May he be seen more clearly by his people and therefore worshiped more truly.

Notes

Chapter 1 The Source and Purpose of Power

1. Diane M. Langberg, *Counseling Survivors of Sexual Abuse* (Maitland, FL: Xulon, 2003).

2. Unless otherwise indicated, Scripture quotations are the author's paraphrase.

Chapter 3 The Role of Deception in the Abuse of Power

1. Joe R. Lansdale, *The Thicket* (New York: Mulholland, 2013), 265.

2. Diane M. Langberg, *Suffering and the Heart of God: How Trauma Destroys and Christ Restores* (Greensboro, NC: New Growth, 2015), 198.

3. Howard Thurman, *Jesus and the Disinherited* (Boston: Beacon, 1976), 55.

4. Elie Wiesel, *Night* (New York: Hill and Wang, 2006), 32–33.

5. Robert Downen, Lise Olsen, and John Tedesco, "Abuse of Faith," *Houston Chronicle*, February 10, 2019, https://www.houstonchronicle.com/news/investigations/article/Southern-Baptist-sexual-abuse-spreads-as-leaders-13588038.php.

6. G. Campbell Morgan, *Studies in the Prophecy of Jeremiah* (Westwood, NJ: Revell, 1955), 99.

7. Handley C. Moule, *The Epistle to the Romans* (Fort Washington, PA: CLC, 1958), 69.

Chapter 4 The Power of Culture and the Influence of Words

1. George MacDonald, *Unspoken Sermon Series III: Kingship* (London: Longmans, Green & Co., 1889), 495.

2. Adolf Hitler, "Adolf Hitler Collection of Speeches 1922–1945," Internet Archive, https://archive.org/stream/AdolfHitlerCollectionOfSpeeches1922194 5/Adolf%20Hitler%20-%20Collection%20of%20Speeches%201922-1945_dj vu.txt.

3. Hitler, "Adolf Hitler Collection of Speeches 1922–1945."

4. "Penn State Scandal Fast Facts," CNN, November 27, 2019, https://www
.cnn.com/2013/10/28/us/penn-state-scandal-fast-facts/index.html.

Chapter 5 Understanding Abuse of Power

1. "Bullying, Cyberbullying, and Suicide Statistics," Megan Meier Foundation,
June 5, 2019, https://meganmeierfoundation.org/statistics.

2. MaryCatherine McDonald, Marisa Brandt, and Robyn Bluhm, "From Shell-
Shock to PTSD, a Century of Invisible War Trauma," *The Conversation*, April
3, 2017, http://theconversation.com/from-shell-shock-to-ptsd-a-century-of-in
visible-war-trauma-74911.

3. Kerry Howley, "Everyone Believed Larry Nassar: The Predatory Trainer
May Just Have Taken Down USA Gymnastics. How Did He Deceive So Many
for So Long?," *The Cut*, November 19, 2018, https://www.thecut.com/2018/11
/how-did-larry-nassar-deceive-so-many-for-so-long.html.

4. Diane M. Langberg, *Counseling Survivors of Sexual Abuse* (Maitland,
FL: Xulon, 2003); and Diane M. Langberg, *On the Threshold of Hope* (Carol
Stream, IL: Tyndale, 1999).

5. "Sexual Assault in the United States," National Sexual Violence Resource
Center, https://www.nsvrc.org/node/4737.

6. Abby Perry, "Prophetic Survivors: Kenny Stubblefield," *Fathom*, October
22, 2018, https://www.fathommag.com/stories/prophetic-survivors-kenny-stub
blefield.

7. Perry, "Prophetic Survivors."

8. Perry, "Prophetic Survivors."

Chapter 6 Power in Human Systems

1. David Crary, "More than 12,000 Boy Scout Members Were Victims of Sexual
Abuse, Expert Says," *Salt Lake Tribune*, April 24, 2019, https://www.sltrib.com
/news/nation-world/2019/04/24/nearly-boy-scout-leaders.

2. Josh Voorhees, "Slatest PM: The Boy Scouts 'Perversion Files,'" *Slate*, October 18, 2012, https://slate.com/news-and-politics/2012/10/boy-scouts-pervers
ion-files-public-database-details-decades-of-alleged-sexual-abuse-cover-up.html.

3. Peter Janci, Twitter post, April 24, 2019, 7:38 a.m., https://twitter.com/pb
janci/status/1121060873076797440.

4. Lauren Bohn, "'We're All Handcuffed in This Country': Why Afghanistan
Is Still the Worst Place in the World to Be a Woman," *Time*, December 8, 2018,
https://time.com/5472411/afghanistan-women-justice-war; and Najim Rahim and
David Zucchino, "Attacks on Girls' Schools on the Rise as Taliban Make Gains,"
New York Times, May 21, 2019, https://www.nytimes.com/2019/05/21/world/asia
/taliban-girls-schools.html.

5. Booker T. Washington, *Up from Slavery* (New York: Doubleday, 1907).

Chapter 7 Power between Men and Women

1. Ruth Tucker and Walter Liefeld, *Daughters of the Church* (Grand Rapids:
Zondervan, 1987), 116.

2. John Knox, *Knox: On Rebellion*, ed. Roger A. Mason (Cambridge: Cambridge University Press, 1994), 9.

3. Thomas Aquinas, *Summa Theologiae*, NewAdvent.org, http://www.new advent.org/summa/1092.htm, question 92, answer 1.

4. Marg Mowczko, "Misogynistic Quotations from Church Fathers and Reformers," *Marg Mowczko* (blog), January 24, 2013, https://margmowczko.com /misogynist-quotes-from-church-fathers.

5. Mowczko, "Misogynistic Quotations."

6. "Harvey Weinstein Sexual Abuse Allegations," Wikipedia, October 6, 2019, https://en.wikipedia.org/wiki/Harvey_Weinstein_sexual_abuse_allegations.

7. Kevin Giles, *The Rise and Fall of the Complementarian Doctrine of the Trinity* (Eugene, OR: Cascade, 2017).

8. Elaine Storkey, *Scars across Humanity: Understanding and Overcoming Violence against Women* (Downers Grove, IL: InterVarsity, 2018).

9. Storkey, *Scars across Humanity*.

Chapter 8 The Intersection of Race and Power

1. James Baldwin, *Notes of a Native Son* (Boston: Beacon, 1955), 30.

2. Mark A. Noll, "Battle for the Bible," *RPM Magazine* 15 (2013): 26, https:// thirdmill.org/articles/mar_noll/mar_noll.BB.html.

3. Melton A. McLaurin, *Celia, a Slave* (Athens: University of Georgia Press, 1991).

4. Isabel Wilkerson, *The Warmth of Other Suns: The Epic Story of America's Great Migration* (New York: Random House, 2010), 418.

5. "Transgenerational Trauma," Wikipedia, September 27, 2019, https:// en.wikipedia.org/wiki/Transgenerational_trauma.

6. Diane Langberg, Twitter post, September 19, 2019, 4:49 a.m., https://twit ter.com/DianeLangberg/status/1174651695953002496.

Chapter 9 Power Abused in the Church

1. Edwin Friedman, *Generation to Generation: Family Process in Church and Synagogue* (New York: Guilford, 1985).

2. Gerben A. Kleef, C. Oveis, I. van der Löwe, A. LuoKogan, J. Goetz, and D. Keltner, "Power, Distress and Compassion," *Psychological Science* 19, no. 12 (2008): 1315–22.

3. Dacher Keltner, Deborah H. Gruenfeld, and Cameron Anderson, "Power, Approach and Inhibition," *Psychological Review* 110, no. 2 (2003): 265–84.

4. Keltner, Gruenfeld, and Anderson, "Power, Approach and Inhibition."

5. Diane Langberg, Twitter post, December 31, 2018, 11:54 a.m., https://twit ter.com/DianeLangberg/status/1079828249092517894.

6. Henry Burton, *The Expositor's Bible: The Gospel according to Luke* (London: Hodder & Stoughton, 1890), 114.

7. Wilhelm Gesenius, *A Hebrew and English Lexicon of the Old Testament*, 4th ed. (Boston: Crocker and Brewster, 1850), 435.

8. G. Campbell Morgan, *The Gospel according to Matthew* (New York: Revell, 1939), 251–52.

Chapter 10 Christendom Seduced by Power

1. Oswald Chambers, *My Utmost for His Highest* (New York: Dodd, Mead & Co., 1935), 18.
2. Chambers, *My Utmost for His Highest*, 6.
3. George MacDonald, *Unspoken Sermon Series III: Kingship* (London: Longmans, Green & Co., 1889), 560.

Chapter 11 Redemptive Power and the Person of Christ

1. Miroslav Volf, "In Light of the Paris Attacks, Is It Time to Eradicate Religion?," *Washington Post*, November 16, 2015, https://www.washingtonpost.com /news/acts-of-faith/wp/2015/11/16/in-light-of-the-paris-attacks-is-it-time-to -eradicate-religion.
2. Oswald Chambers, *Disciples Indeed* (Grand Rapids: Discovery House, 1955), 393.
3. Amy Carmichael, *If* (Fort Washington, PA: CLC, 2012), 13.
4. Meredith Somers, "More than Half of Christian Men Admit to Watching Pornography," *Washington Times*, August 24, 2014, https://www.washington times.com/news/2014/aug/24/more-than-half-of-christian-men-admit-to-watch ing-/.
5. "New Marriage and Divorce Statistics Released," Barna Group, March 31, 2008, https://www.barna.com/research/new-marriage-and-divorce-statistics -released.
6. "What Is the Church's Role in Racial Reconciliation?," Barna Group, July 20, 2019, https://www.barna.com/research/racial-reconciliation/.
7. C. H. Spurgeon, *Return, O Shulamite! And Other Sermons Preached in 1884* (New York: Carter, 1885), 174.
8. Dietrich Bonhoeffer, *Life Together: The Classic Exploration of Christian Community* (New York: Harper & Row, 1954), 107.
9. Dietrich Bonhoeffer, *Letters and Paper from Prison* (New York: MacMillan, 1959), 369.

Chapter 12 Healing Power and the Body of Christ

1. C. S. Lewis, *Mere Christianity* (New York: HarperOne, 1952), 92.
2. George MacDonald, *Unspoken Sermon Series III: Kingship* (London: Longmans, Green & Co., 1889), 420–21.
3. Amy Carmichael, *From Sunrise Land: Letters from Japan* (London: Marshall Brothers, 1895), 76.
4. George Matheson, *The Lady Ecclesia: An Autobiography* (New York: Dodd, Mead & Co., 1897).
5. Jennifer Viegas, "Infanticide Common in Roman Empire," NBC, May 5, 2011, http://www.nbcnews.com/id/42911813/ns/technology_and_science-science /t/infanticide-common-roman-empire/#.XZ-o7-dKgWp.

6. Diane M. Langberg, *Suffering and the Heart of God: How Trauma Destroys and Christ Restores* (Greensboro, NC: New Growth, 2015), 7.

7. Jake Griesel, "Aristides of Athens (2nd century AD) on the Conduct of Christians," *Theological est doctrina Deo vivendi per Christum Jacobi Grieselli Blogus theologicus*, December 31, 2013, https://deovivendiperchristum.word press.com/2013/12/31/aristides-of-athens-2nd-century-ad-on-the-conduct-of -christians.

8. G. Campbell Morgan, *Hosea: The Heart and Holiness of God* (London: Marshall, Morgan & Scott, 1948), 29.

Postlude

1. Elie Wiesel, *Night* (New York: Hill and Wang, 2006), 41–42.

2. Wiesel, *Night*, 33.

Acknowledgments

1. George MacDonald, *Unspoken Sermon Series III: The Inheritance* (London: Longmans, Green & Co., 1889), 613–14.

Author Bio

Diane Langberg (PhD, Temple University) is an internationally recognized psychologist and counselor with forty-seven years of experience. She speaks regularly on abuse and trauma all over the world; directs her own counseling practice in Jenkintown, Pennsylvania; and cofounded the Global Trauma Recovery Institute at Missio Seminary in Philadelphia. Langberg is also on the board of GRACE (Godly Response to Abuse in a Christian Environment), led by Boz Tchividjian, and cochairs the American Bible Society's Trauma Advisory Counsel. She has authored or coauthored numerous books, including *Counseling Survivors of Sexual Abuse*, *On the Threshold of Hope*, and *Suffering the Heart of God: How Trauma Destroys and Christ Restores*.